Microsoft Office
for Beginners

M.L. HUMPHREY

SELECT TITLES BY M.L. HUMPHREY

EXCEL ESSENTIALS
Excel for Beginners
Intermediate Excel
50 Useful Excel Functions
50 More Excel Functions

ACCESS ESSENTIALS
Access for Beginners
Intermediate Access

WORD ESSENTIALS
Word for Beginners
Intermediate Word

POWERPOINT ESSENTIALS
PowerPoint for Beginners
Intermediate PowerPoint

BUDGETING FOR BEGINNERS
Budgeting for Beginners
Excel for Budgeting

CONTENTS

INTRODUCTION

This book includes the content of three separate titles, *Excel for Beginners, Word for Beginners, and PowerPoint for Beginners*, which are in my mind the three main Microsoft Office programs. By the time you finish this book you should be able to comfortably work in all three at a solid beginner level. That means opening each program and performing normal, everyday tasks.

As you work through this book you'll start to see that all Microsoft Office programs operate from the same basic foundation and that they share the same structure and many of the same shortcuts, so being familiar with one program will help you to learn the others.

The screenshots and instructions in this book are written based on Microsoft Office 2013. For anyone using Office 2007 or later you should be able to do anything covered here even if you're using a different version of Office. Yes, Microsoft does release new versions of Office on a regular basis, but the changes they tend to make are to the more advanced functions. Since these books cover the basic building blocks of Office, those rarely change over time.

(As a matter of fact, the only major change I recall happening in the twenty-five years I've been using Microsoft Office was that switch to Office 2007 that drastically changed the appearance of all of the programs and moved everything around. But even then the Ctrl shortcuts and many of the right-click dropdown menus stayed the same.)

Since these books were originally written to standalone, there will be some overlap in the introductions for each where terminology is discussed, but it's still a good idea to read each title from start to finish.

Good luck with it. Reach out if you get stuck.

Excel for Beginners

EXCEL ESSENTIALS BOOK 1

M.L. HUMPHREY

CONTENTS

INTRODUCTION

The purpose of this guide is to introduce you to the basics of using Microsoft Excel. I still remember when I was in college and helping a graduate student do research and he asked me to do something in Excel and I had no idea what to do and how frustrating that was to be limited by my lack of knowledge. I was later fortunate enough to work with a man who was absolutely brilliant with Excel who taught me lots of tips and tricks for using it and now I don't know what I'd do without it.

Excel is great. I use it both in my professional life and my personal life. It allows me to organize and track key information in a quick and easy manner and to automate a lot of the calculations I need. I have a budget worksheet that I look at at least every few days to track whether my bills have been paid and how much I need to keep in my bank account and just where I am overall financially. In my professional career I've used it in a number of ways, from analyzing a series of financial transactions to see if a customer was overcharged to performing a comparison of regulatory requirements across multiple jurisdictions. While it works best for numerical purposes, it is often a good choice for text-based analysis as well, especially if you want to be able to sort your results or filter out and isolate certain results.

If you want to learn Excel through the lens of managing your own money, the *Juggling Your Finances: Basic Excel Primer*, is probably a better choice. It walks you through how to do addition, subtraction, multiplication, and division using key questions you should be able to answer about your personal finances as the examples.

This book just focuses on the basics of using Excel without those kinds of specific examples. We'll cover how to navigate Excel, input data, format it, manipulate it through basic math formulas, filter it, sort it, and print your results.

This is not a comprehensive Excel guide. We are not going to cover more complex topics like conditional formatting and pivot tables. The goal of this guide is to give you a solid grounding in Excel that will let you get started using it. For day-to-day uses, this guide should cover 98% of what you need and I'll give you some tips on how to find the other 2 percent. (Or you can continue on with *Intermediate Excel* which covers more advanced topics like pivot tables, charts, conditional formatting, and IF functions.)

One note before we start: I'm working in Excel 2013, which will look familiar to users of Excel 2007 or later. If you're working in a version of Excel that's pre-2007, I'd recommend that you upgrade now rather than try to learn Excel in an older version. They're different enough that it's really like a completely different program.

If you do insist on using an older version of Excel, when I give you more than one method you can use (sometimes there are at least three ways to do the same thing in Excel), choose the option that tells you to right-click and open a dialogue box. Also, the Ctrl + [letter] options should be available in all versions of Excel. If that fails, use the help function to search for how the task can be completed in your version.

Alright then. Let's get started.

BASIC TERMINOLOGY

First things first, we need to establish some basic terminology so that you know what I'm talking about when I refer to a cell or a row or a column, etc.

Column

Excel uses columns and rows to display information. Columns run across the top of the worksheet and, unless you've done something funky with your settings, are identified using letters of the alphabet. As you can see below, they start with A on the far left side and march right on through the alphabet (A, B, C, D, E, etc.). If you scroll far enough to the right, you'll see that they continue on to a double alphabet (AA, AB, AC, etc.).

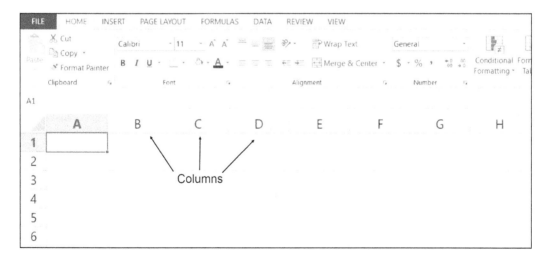

Row

Rows run down the side of the worksheet and are numbered starting at 1 and up to a very high number. You can hold down the ctrl key in a blank worksheet while hitting the down arrow to see just how many rows your version of Excel has. Mine has 65,536 rows per worksheet.

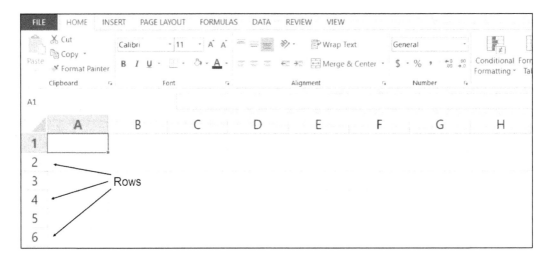

Cell

A cell is a combination of a column and row that is identified by the letter of the column it's in and the number of the row it's in. For example, Cell A1 is the cell in the first column and the first row of the worksheet. When you've clicked on a specific cell it will have a darker border around the edges like in the image below.

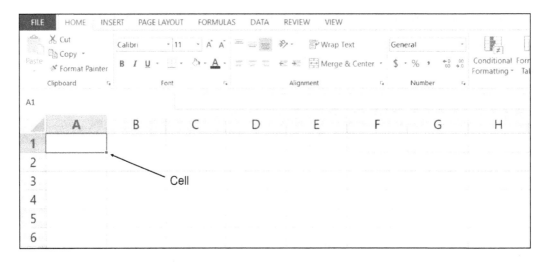

Click

If I tell you to click on something, that means to use your mouse (or trackpad) to move the arrow on the screen over to a specific location and left-click or right-click on the option. (See the next definition for the difference between left-click and right-click).

If you left-click, this selects the item. If you right-click, this generally creates a dropdown list of options to choose from. If I don't tell you which to do, left- or right-click, then left-click.

Left-click/Right-click

If you look at your mouse or your trackpad, you generally have two flat buttons to press. One is on the left side, one is on the right. If I say left-click that means to press down on the button on the left. If I say right-click that means press down on the button on the right. (If you're used to using Word or Excel you may already do this without even thinking about it. So, if that's the case then think of left-click as what you usually use to select text and right-click as what you use to see a menu of choices.)

Now, as I sadly learned when I had to upgrade computers and ended up with an HP Envy, not all track pads have the left- and right-hand buttons. In that case, you'll basically want to press on either the bottom left-hand side of the track pad or the bottom right-hand side of the trackpad. Since you're working blind it may take a little trial and error to get the option you want working. (Or is that just me?)

Spreadsheet

I'll try to avoid using this term, but if I do use it, I'll mean your entire Excel file. It's a little confusing because it can sometimes also be used to mean a specific worksheet, which is why I'll try to avoid it as much as possible.

Worksheet

A worksheet is basically a combination of rows and columns that you can enter data in. When you open an Excel file, it opens to worksheet one.

My version of Excel has one worksheet available by default when I open a new Excel file. (It's possible to add more as needed.) That worksheet is labeled Sheet 1 and the name is highlighted in white to show that it's in use.

Formula Bar

This is the long white bar at the top of the screen with the $f\chi$ symbol next to it. If you click in a cell and start typing, you'll see that what you type appears not only in that cell, but in the formula bar. When you input a formula into a cell and then hit enter, the value returned by the formula will be what displays in the cell, but the formula will appear in the formula bar when you have that cell highlighted.

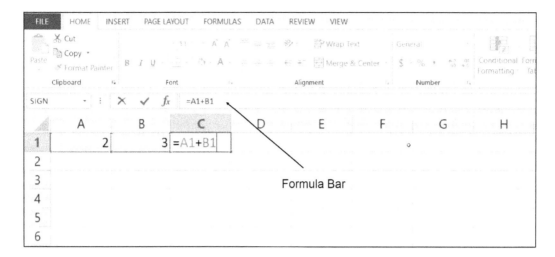

Formula Bar

Tab

I refer to the menu choices at the top of the screen (File, Home, Insert, Page Layout, Formulas, Data, Review and View) as tabs. Note how they look like folder tabs from an old-time filing system when selected? That's why.

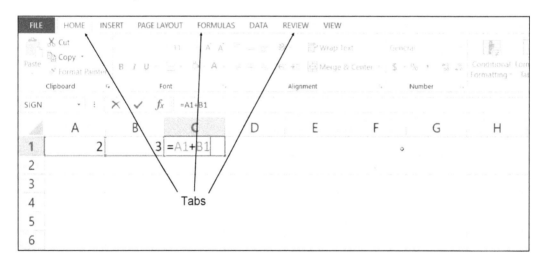

Tabs

Each menu tab you select will show you different options. On my Home tab I can do things like copy/cut/paste, format cells, edit cells, and insert/delete cells, for example. (This is one place where things are very different for those using earlier versions of Excel and why if you're using an older version of Excel, I'd recommend upgrading now.)

Scroll Bar

On the right side and the bottom of the screen are two bars with arrows at the ends. If you left-click and hold on either bar you can move it back and forth between those arrows (or up and down for the one on the right side). This lets you see information that's off the page in your current view but part of the worksheet you're viewing.

You can also use the arrows at the ends of the scroll bar to do the same thing. Left-click on the arrow once to move it one line or column or left-click and hold to get it to move as far as it can go. If you want to cover more rows/columns at a time you can click into the blank space on either side of the scroll bar to move an entire screen at a time, assuming you have enough data entered for that.

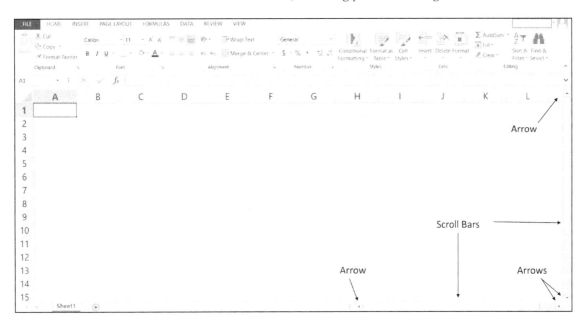

Using the arrows instead of clicking on the scroll bar lets you scroll all the way to the far end of the worksheet. Using the scroll bars only lets you move to the end of the information you've already entered.

Data

I use data and information interchangeably. Whatever information you put into a worksheet is your data.

Table

I may also refer to a table of data or data table on occasion. This is just a combination of rows and columns that contain information.

Select

If I tell you to "select" cells, that means to highlight them. If the cells are next to each other, you can just left-click on the first one and drag the cursor (move your mouse or finger on the trackpad) until all of the cells are highlighted. When this happens, they'll all be surrounded by a dark box like below.

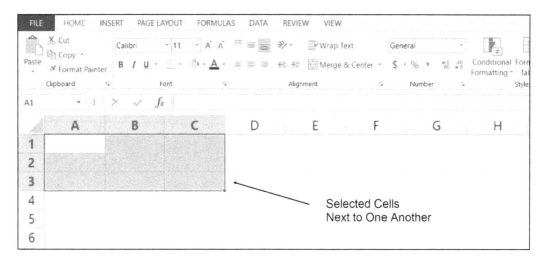

Selected Cells
Next to One Another

If the cells aren't next to each other, then what you do is left-click on the first cell, hold down the Ctrl key (bottom left of my keyboard), left-click on the next cell, hold down the Ctrl key, left-click on the next cell, etc. until you've selected all the cells you want. The cells you've already selected will be shaded in gray and the one you selected last will be surrounded by a dark border that is not as dark as the normal border you see when you just select one cell. In the image below cells A1, C1, A3, and C3 are selected.

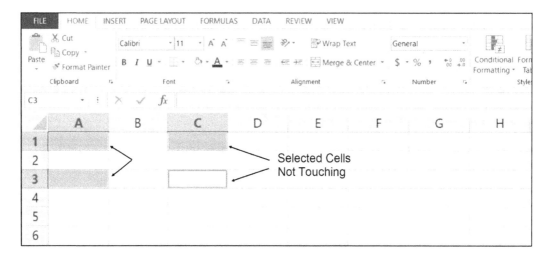

Selected Cells
Not Touching

Dropdown

I will occasionally refer to a dropdown or dropdown menu. This is generally a list of potential choices that you can select from. The existence of the list is indicated by an arrow next to the first available selection.

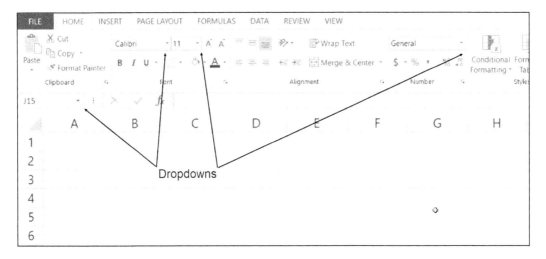

I will also sometimes refer to the list of options you see when you click on a dropdown arrow as the dropdown menu.

Dialogue Box

Dialogue boxes are pop-up boxes that contain a set of available options and appear when you need to provide additional information or make additional choices. For example, this is the Insert dialogue box that appears when you choose to insert a cell:

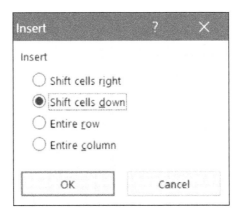

Cursor

If you didn't know this one already, it's what moves around when you move the mouse (or use the trackpad). In Excel it often looks like a three-dimensional squat cross or it will look like one of a couple of varieties of arrow. (Open Excel and move it to where the column and row labels are to see what I mean.) The different shapes the cursor takes represent different functions.

Arrow

If I say that you can "arrow" to something that just means to use the arrow keys to navigate from one cell to another. For example, if you enter information in A1 and hit enter, that moves your cursor down to cell A2. If instead you wanted to move to Cell B1, you could do so with the right arrow.

ABSOLUTE BASICS

It occurs to me that there are a few absolute basics to using Excel that we should cover before we get into things like formatting.

Opening an Excel File

To start a brand new Excel file, I simply click on Excel 2013 from my applications menu or the shortcut I have on my computer's taskbar, and it opens a new Excel file for me.

If you're opening an existing Excel file, you can either go to the folder where the file is saved and double-click on the file name, or you can (if Excel is already open) go to the File tab and choose Open from the left-hand menu.

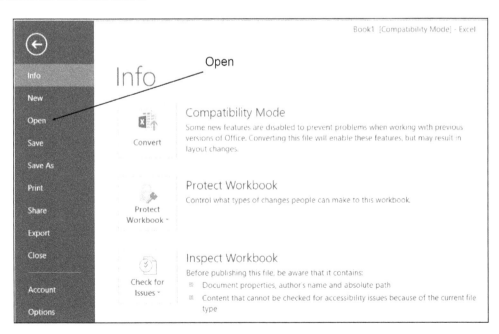

That will show you a list of Recent Workbooks. If it includes the one you're looking for, you can just click on it once and it will open.

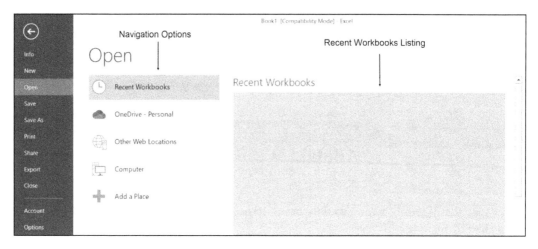

If you don't see the file you're looking for, you can click on the list of navigation options in between the left-hand menu and the list of Recent Workbooks and navigate to where the file is stored. When I click on Computer it gives me the current folder I'm in as well as five recent folders and an option to browse if the folder I want isn't one of the ones displayed.

Saving an Excel File

To save a file you can go to the File tab at the top of the screen and then choose Save or Save As from the menu options on the left side.

When you're dealing with a new Excel file, you really only have the Save As option. (When I click on Save it still takes me to Save As.) With Save As, Excel will ask you to choose which folder to save the file into. You can either choose from the list of recent folders on the right-hand side or navigate to the folder you want using the locations listing on the left of that list.

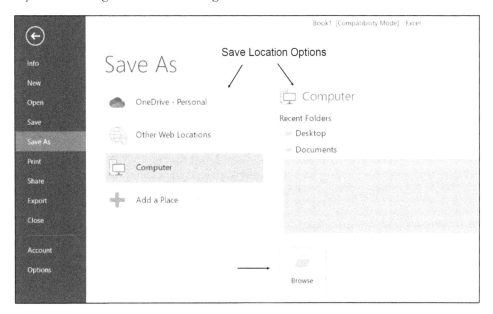

Once you choose a location, a dialogue box will appear where you can name the file.

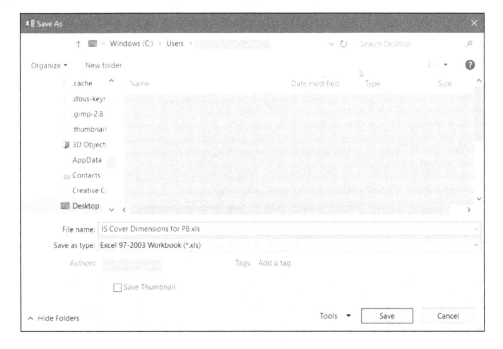

My save options default to an .xls file type. I don't know if this is standard or if I've set it up that way somewhere. If yours doesn't default to the .xls file type, I'd recommend using that file type as much as possible if you think you might share the file at any point. The newer versions of Excel actually are an .xlsx file type, but if you use that file type and want to share with someone who has a version of Excel that's pre-2007, they won't be able to open your file.

It's much easier to save down to an older version than have to convert up to a newer version. And I'm pretty sure if you're using this guide you won't be using any of the fancy options that are available in the newest versions of Excel that aren't available in older versions. If it turns out you are, Excel will generate a warning message about compatibility when you save the file as an .xls file, and you can decide not to save it to the older version at that time.

If you're saving a file you've already saved once before and you have no changes to its name, location, or type, you can go to File>Save and it will save it for you, keeping all of that information the same. You can also just type Ctrl and S at the same time (Ctrl+S) (Note: Even though I'm going to show these commands with a capital letter, you don't have to use the capitalized version of the letter.)

Or, and I think this is true of all Excel users, there should be a small computer disk image in the top left corner that you can click on. (You can customize that list and I have for my most-used functions, which is why I'm not 100% sure.)

If you're saving a file you've already saved once before but you want to save it to a new location, change its name, or change the file type (.xls to .xlsx, for example), use Save As.

Deleting an Excel File

You can't delete an Excel file from within Excel. You'll need to navigate to the folder where the file is stored and delete the file there without opening it. First, click on the file name. (Only enough to select it. Make sure you haven't double-clicked and highlighted the name which will then try to rename the file.) Next, choose Delete from the menu at the top of the screen, or right-click and choose Delete from the dropdown menu.

Renaming an Excel File

You might want to rename an Excel file at some point. You can Save As and choose a new name for the file, but that will mean you now have two versions of the file, one with the old name and one with the new name. Or you can navigate to where you've saved the file, click on it once to highlight the file, click on it a second time to highlight the name, and then type in the new name you want to use. If you do it that way, there will only be one version of the file, the one with the name you wanted.

If you do rename a file, know that you can't then access it from the Recent Workbooks listing under Open file. Even though it might be listed there, Excel won't be able to find it because it no longer has that name. (Same thing happens if you move a file from the location it was in when you were last working on it. I often run into this by moving a file into a new subfolder when I suddenly get inspired to organize my records.)

NAVIGATING EXCEL

The next thing we're going to discuss is basic navigation within Excel. These are all things you can do that don't involve inputting, formatting, or manipulating your data.

Basic Navigation Within A Worksheet

Excel will automatically open into cell A1 of Sheet 1 for a new Excel file. For an existing file it will open in the cell and worksheet where you were when you last saved the file. (This means it can also open with a set of cells already highlighted if that's what you were doing when you last saved the file.)

Within a worksheet, it's pretty basic to navigate.

You can click into any cell you can see in the worksheet with your mouse or trackpad. Just place your cursor over the cell and left-click.

From the cell where you currently are (which will be outlined with a dark border), you can use the up, down, left, and right arrow keys to move one cell in any of those directions.

You can also use the tab key to move one cell to the right and the shift and tab keys combined (shift + tab) to move one cell to the left.

To see other cells in the worksheet that aren't currently visible, you can use the scroll bars on the right-hand side or the bottom of the worksheet. The right-hand-side scroll bar will let you move up and down. The bottom scroll bar will let you move right or left. Just remember that the bars themselves will only let you move as far as you've entered data, you need to use the arrows at the ends of the scroll bars to move farther than that.

For worksheets with lots of data in them, click on the scroll bar and drag it to move quickly to the beginning or end of the data. To move one view's worth at a time, click in the blank space around the actual bar.

If you're using the scroll bars to navigate, remember that until you click into a new cell with your mouse or trackpad you will still be in the last cell where you clicked or made an edit. (You can test this by typing and you'll see that you're brought back to that last cell, wherever it is.)

Basic Navigation Between Worksheets

Between worksheets, you can either click on the name of the worksheet you want (at the bottom of the screen) or you can use Ctrl and Page Up (Ctrl + Page Up) to move one worksheet to the left and Ctrl and Page Down (Ctrl + Page Dn) to move one worksheet to the right.

F2

If you click in a cell and hit the F2 key, this will take you to the end of the contents of the cell. This can be very useful when you need to edit the contents of a cell or to work with a formula in that cell.

Insert a Cell in a Worksheet

(See the next section for how to insert an entire row or column.) Sometimes you just want to insert one cell in the worksheet. To do so, click on where you want to insert the cell, right-click, and select Insert.

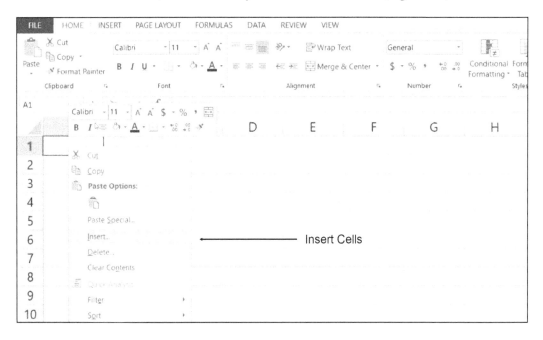

You'll be given four choices, Shift Cells Right, Shift Cells Down, Entire Row, and Entire Column.

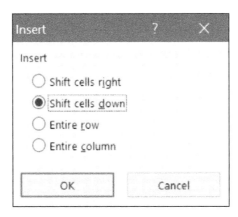

Shift Cells Right will insert your cell by moving every other cell in that row to the right. Shift Cells Down will insert your cell by moving every other cell in that column down. Entire row will insert an entire row instead of one cell. Entire column will insert an entire column instead of one cell.

Be sure that the option you choose makes sense given the other data you've already entered in the worksheet. Sometimes I find that I need to actually highlight a group of cells and insert cells for all of them to keep the rest of my cells aligned.

You can also highlight the cell(s) where you want to insert cell(s) and then go to the Cells section of the Home tab where it says Insert. Choose the insert option you want from there, the same way you would for inserting a worksheet.

Insert a Column or Row

Sometimes you'll enter information and then realize that you want to add an entire row or column right in the midst of the data you've already entered. If this happens, highlight the row or column where you want your new row or column to go, right-click, and select Insert. (By highlight, I mean click on either the letter of the column or the number of the row to select the entire column or row.) Your data will either shift one entire column to the right or one entire row downward, starting with the column or row you selected.

You can also just click in one cell and then choose Entire Row or Entire Column after right-clicking and choosing Insert.

Another option is to highlight the row or column and then go to the Cells section of the Home tab where it says Insert and choose the insert option you want from there.

Insert a New Worksheet

When you open a new Excel file, you'll have one worksheet you can use named Sheet 1. (In Excel 2007 I had three worksheets available when I opened a new file.)

If you need another worksheet, simply click on the + symbol in a circle at the end of your existing worksheets to add a new one. (In Excel 2007 the add a worksheet option looked like a mini worksheet with a yellow star in the corner.)

You can also go to the Home tab under the Cells section and left-click the arrow under Insert then select Insert Sheet from the dropdown menu.

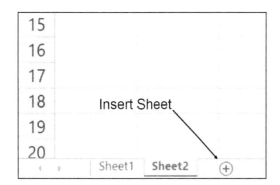

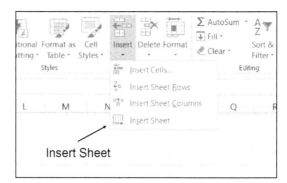

Delete a Cell in a Worksheet

Deleting a cell in a worksheet is a lot like inserting a cell. Right-click on the cell you want to delete and choose Delete from the dropdown menu. Next choose whether to shift cells up or left. (When you remove a cell everything will have to move to fill in the empty space it leaves.) Be sure that deleting that one cell doesn't change the layout of the rest of your data. As with inserting a cell, I sometimes find I need to delete more than one cell to keep things uniform in my presentation.

(Note that you can also delete an entire row or column this way as well.)

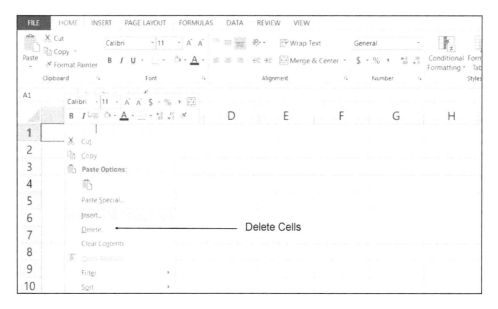

Another option is to highlight the cell(s) you want to delete, and then go to the Cells section of the Home tab where it says Delete and choose the delete option you want from there.

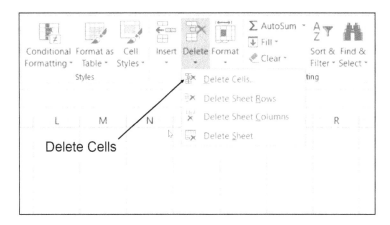

Delete Cells

Delete a Column or Row

Highlight the entire row or column you want to delete, right-click, and select Delete. It will automatically delete the row or column. You can also highlight the row or column and then go to the Cells section of the Home tab where it says Delete and choose the delete option you want from there. And, as with inserting a row or column, you can click into one cell, right-click, select Delete, and then choose Entire Row or Entire Column from the dialogue box.

Delete a Worksheet

Sometimes you'll add a worksheet and then realize you don't want it anymore. It's easy enough to delete. Just right-click on the name of the worksheet you want to delete and choose the Delete option from the dropdown menu.

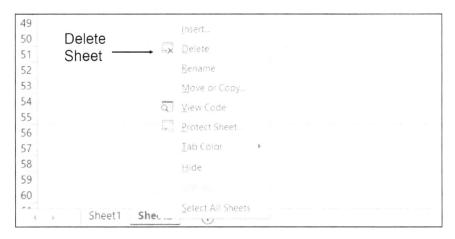

Delete Sheet

You can also go to the Cells section in the Home tab, left-click on the arrow under Delete, and choose Delete Sheet from the dropdown menu.

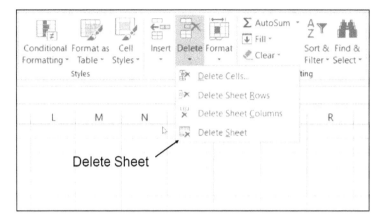

Delete Sheet

If there was any data in the worksheet you're trying to delete, it will give you a warning message to that effect. If you don't care, click Delete. If you didn't realize there was data and want to cancel the deletion, click Cancel.

Be sure you want to delete any worksheet you choose to delete, because you can't get it back later. This is one place where undo will not work.

Rename A Worksheet

The default name for worksheets in Excel are Sheet 1, Sheet 2, Sheet 3, etc. They're not useful for much of anything, and if you have information in more than one worksheet, you're going to want to rename them to something that lets you identify which worksheet is which.

If you double left-click on a worksheet name (on the tab at the bottom) it will highlight in gray and you can then delete the existing name and replace it with whatever you want.

You can also right-click on the tab name and choose Rename from the dropdown menu.

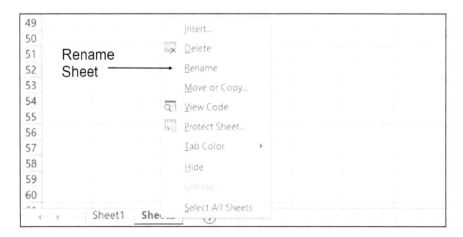

Rename Sheet

A worksheet name cannot be more than 31 characters long, be blank, contain the forward slash, the back slash, a question mark, a star, a colon, or brackets (/ \ ? * : [ ]), begin or end with an apostrophe, or be named History. Don't worry. In my version of Excel it just stops you from typing those characters or past the limit. (In earlier versions I believe it let you type the incorrect characters and then gave an error message and refused to accept the name.)

INPUTTING YOUR DATA

At its most basic, inputting your data is very simple. Click in the cell where you want to input information and type. But there are some tricks to it that you'll want to keep in mind.

First, let's take a step back and talk about one of the key strengths of a using Excel and that's the ability to sort or filter your data. For example, I self-publish books, and every month I get reports from the places where my books are published listing all of the sales of my books at those locations. But what if I only care about the sales of book A? How can I see those if I have a couple hundred rows of information in the report they've given me?

Well, if the site where I sold those books is nice and helpful and they understand data analysis, they've given me my sales listings in an Excel worksheet with one header row at the top and then one row for each sale or each book. If they've done that, then I can very easily filter my data on the title column and see just the entries related to title A. If they haven't, then I'm stuck deleting rows of information I don't need to get to the data I want.

Which is all a roundabout way of saying that you can input your data any way you want, but if you follow some key data principles you'll have a lot more flexibility in what you can do with your data once it's entered.

Those principles are:

1. Use the first row of your worksheet to label your data.

2. List all of your data in continuous rows after that first row without including any subtotals or subheadings or anything that isn't your data.

3. To the extent possible, format your data in such a way that it can be analyzed. (So rather than put in a free-text field, try to use a standardized list of values instead. See below. Column E, which uses a 1 to 5 point ranking scale, is better for analysis than Column D, which is a free text field where anyone can say anything.)

4. Standardize your values. Customer A should always be listed as Customer A. United States should always be United States not USA, U.S.A., or America.

5. Store your raw data in one location; analyze or correct it elsewhere.

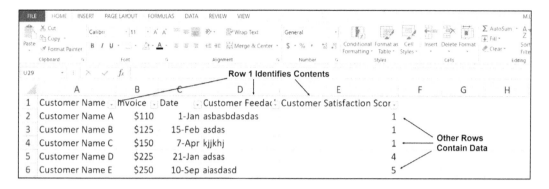

Now, I'm saying all of this, but some of the ways I use Excel don't conform to these principles. And that's fine. My budgeting worksheet is not meant to be filtered or sorted. It's a snapshot of information that summarizes my current financial position. But my worksheet that lists all vendor payments for the year? You bet it's formatted using this approach.

So before you enter any data into your Excel file, put some time into thinking about how you want to use that data. Is it just a visual snapshot? If so, don't worry about structuring it for sorting or filtering. Will it be hundreds of rows of values that you want to summarize or analyze? If so, then arrange it the way I listed above. You don't have to have row 1 be your column headings, but wherever you put those headings, keep everything below that point single rows of data that are all formatted and entered using the same definitions.

Okay. So what are some tricks to make entering your information easier?

Undo

If you enter the wrong information or perform the wrong action and want to easily undo it, hold down the Ctrl key and the Z key at the same time. (Ctrl + Z) You can do this multiple times if you want to undo multiple actions, although there are a few actions (such as deleting a worksheet) that cannot be undone.

Redo

If you mistakenly undo something and want it back, you can hold down the Ctrl key and the Y key at the same time to redo it. (Ctrl + Y)

Auto-Suggested Text

If you've already typed text into a cell, Excel will suggest that text to you in subsequent cells in the same column.

For example, if you are creating a list of all the books you own (something I once tried to do and gave up after about a hundred entries), and in cell A1 you type "science fiction", when you go to cell A2 and type an "s", Excel will automatically suggest to you "science fiction". If you don't want to use that suggestion, then keep typing. If you do, then hit enter.

Nice, huh? Instead of typing fifteen characters you were able to type one.

This only works when you have unique values for Excel to identify. If you have science fiction/fantasy and science fiction as entries in that column, it's not going to work. Excel waits until it can suggest one option, so you'd have to type science fiction/ before it made any suggestions.

Also, if there are empty cells between the entries you already completed and the one you're now completing and you have no other columns with completed data in them that bridge that gap, Excel won't make a suggestion.

Another time it doesn't work is if you have a very long list that you've completed and the matching entry is hundreds of rows away from the one you're now completing.

Excel also doesn't make suggestions for numbers. And if you have an entry that combines letters and numbers, it won't make a suggestion until you've typed at least one letter.

Despite all these apparent limitations, auto-suggested text can be very handy to use if you have to enter one of a limited number of choices over and over again and can't easily copy the information into your worksheet.

Copying the Contents and Formatting of One Cell To Another

This is very easy. Highlight the information you want to copy and hold down the Ctrl and C keys at the same time (Ctrl + C). Go to the cell where you want to put the information you copied and hit Enter.

If you want to copy to more than one location, instead of hitting Enter at the new cell, hold down the Ctrl and V keys at the same time (Ctrl + V). If you use Ctrl + V, you'll see that the original cell you copied from is still surrounded by a dotted line meaning that text is still available to be pasted into another cell.

You can also right-click and select Copy from the dropdown menu and then right-click Paste from the dropdown menu in the cell where you want the information. (In my version of Excel, right-click Paste is now represented by a clipboard with a plain white page under the Paste Options header.)

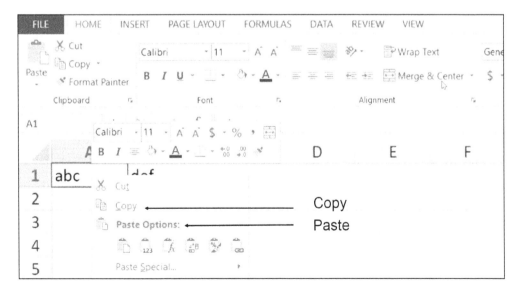

Once you're done pasting the values into new cells and want to do something else, just hit the Esc key. This will remove the dotted line from around the cell you were copying and ensure you don't accidentally paste it somewhere else. Typing in a new cell also works.

Moving the Contents of a Cell (Cutting)

To move the contents of a cell rather than copy it, you select the cell with the contents you want to move, type Ctrl and X at the same time (Ctrl + X), click on the new location, and hit Enter or type Ctrl + V. Unlike with copying, you can only move the contents of a cell to one new location.

Another option is to highlight the cell(s) you want to move, right-click, and choose Cut from the dropdown menu and then paste your cell contents in the new location.

Copying the contents of a cell (Ctrl + C) is different from cutting and moving the contents of a cell (Ctrl + X), because when you copy the contents of a cell they remain in their original location. When you move the contents, you are removing them from their original location to place them in their new location.

Copying Versus Moving When It Comes to Formulas

If you're dealing with text, copying (Ctrl + C) or cutting the text (Ctrl + X) doesn't really change anything. What ends up in that new cell will be the same regardless of the method you use.

But with formulas, that's not what happens.

With formulas, moving the contents of a cell (Ctrl + X) will keep the formula the exact same as it was. So if you're formula was =A2+B2 it will still be =A2+B2 in the new cell.

Copying the contents of a cell (Ctrl + C) will *change the formula* based upon the number of rows and columns you moved. The formula is copied relative to where it originated. If your original formula in cell A3 was =A2+B2 and you copied it to cell A4 (so moved one cell downward) the formula in cell A4 will be =A3+B3. All cell references in the formula will adjust one cell downward.

If you copy that same formula to cell B3 (so one cell to the right) the formula in B3 will be =B2+C2. All cell references in the formula will adjust one cell to the right.

If this doesn't make sense to you, just try it. Put some sample values in cells A2 and B2 and then experiment with Ctrl + C versus Ctrl + X.

Also, there is a way to prevent a formula from changing when you copy it using the $ sign to fix the cell reference. We'll talk about that next.

Copying Formulas To Other Cells While Keeping One Value Fixed

If you want to copy a formula while keeping the value of one or more of the cells fixed, you need to use the $ sign.

A $ sign in front of the letter portion of a cell location will keep the column the same but allow the row number to change. ($A1)

A $ sign in front of the number portion of a cell location will keep the row the same but allow the column to change. (A$1)

A $ sign in front of both will keep the referenced cell exactly the same. (A1)

This is discussed in more detail in the manipulating data section.

Paste Special

Sometimes you want to copy just the contents of a cell without keeping any of its formatting. Or you want to take a list of values in a column and put them into a single row instead.

That's where the Paste Special options come in handy.

First, know that you can only use Paste Special options if you've copied the contents of a cell (Ctrl + C). They don't work if you've cut the contents using Ctrl +X.

To Paste Special, instead of just typing Ctrl + V to paste what you copied into a new cell, right-click in the new cell and choose from the Paste Options section.

You should see in the dropdown menu something like this. What you see will be determined by what you've copied and how.

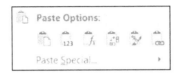

In my opinion, not all of these choices are useful. So I'm just going to highlight two of them for you.

Paste Values, which has the 123 on its clipboard, is useful for when you want the results of a formula, but don't want the formula anymore. I use this often.

It's also useful when you want the contents of a cell, but would prefer to use the formatting from the destination cell(s). For example, if you're copying from one Excel file to another.

Another way I use it is when I've run a set of calculations on my data, found my values, and now want to sort or do something else with my data and don't want to risk having the values change on me. I highlight the entire data set, copy, and then paste special-values right over the top of my existing data. (Just be sure to type Esc after you do this so that the change is fixed in place.)

The Paste Transpose option—the one with the little arrow arcing between two pairs of cells, fourth from the left above—is very useful if you have a row of data that you want to turn into columns of data or vice versa. Just highlight the data, copy, paste-transpose, and it will automatically paste a column of data as a row or a row of data as a column. Just be sure before you paste that there isn't any data already there that will be overwritten, because Excel won't warn you before it overwrites it.

There are more paste options available than just the six you can see above. Click on where it says Paste Special and you'll see another dropdown menu to the side with eight more options, and if you go to the bottom of that breakout menu and click on Paste Special again, it will bring up the Paste Special dialogue box:

Displaying The Contents Of A Cell As Text

Excel likes to change certain values to what it thinks you meant. So if you enter June 2015 into a cell, it will convert that entry to a date even if you intended it to be text.

It also assumes that any entry that starts with a minus sign (-), an equals sign (=), or a plus sign (+) is a formula.

To keep Excel from doing this, you can type a single quote mark (') before the contents of the cell. If you do that, Excel will treat whatever you enter after that as text and will keep the formatting type as General.

So if you want to have June 2015 display in a cell in your worksheet, you need to type 'June 2015.

If you want to have

- Item A

display in a cell, you need to type it as:

'- Item A

The single quote mark is not visible when you look at or print your worksheet. It is only visible in the formula bar when you've selected that cell.

Entering a Formula Into a Cell

The discussion just above about displaying the contents of a cell as text brings up another good point. If you want Excel to treat an entry as a formula then you need to enter the equals (=), plus (+), or negative sign (-) as your first character in the cell.

So, if you type

$$1+1$$

in a cell, that will just display as text in the cell. You'll see

$$1+1.$$

But if you type

$$+1+1$$

in a cell, Excel will treat that as a formula and calculate it. You'll see

$$2$$

in the cell and

$$=1+1$$

in the formula bar. Same with if you type

$$=1+1$$

It will calculate that as a formula, display 2 in the cell, and show =1+1 in the formula bar. If you type

$$-1+1$$

in a cell it will treat that as a formula adding negative 1 to 1 and will show that as 0 in the cell and display

$$=-1+1$$

in the formula bar. Best practice is to just use the equals sign to start every formula.

Including Line Breaks Within a Cell

I sometimes need to have multiple lines of text or numbers within a cell. So instead of a, b, c, I need

a

b

c

You can't just hit Enter, because if you do it'll take you to the next cell. Instead, hold down the Alt key at the same time you hit Enter. This will create a line break within the cell.

Deleting Data

If you enter information into a cell and later decide you want to delete it, you can click on that cell(s) and use the delete button on your computer's keyboard. This will remove whatever you entered in the cell without deleting the cell as well.

You can also double-click into the cell or use F2 to get to the end of the contents and then use your computer's backspace key to delete out the contents of the cell.

Deleting the contents of a cell will not remove its formatting. To delete the contents of a cell as well as its formatting, go to the Editing section of the Home tab, click on the dropdown next to the Clear option, and choose to Clear All.

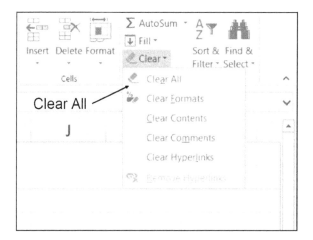

Find and Replace

Sometimes you have a big worksheet and you need to find a specific entry. An easy way to do this is to use the Find option. The easiest way to access it is to type Ctrl and F at the same time (Ctrl + F). This opens the Find dialogue box. Type what you're looking for into the "Find what" field and hit enter. The default is for find to look in formulas as well, so if you search for "f" and have a formula that references cell F11, it will hit on that as much as it will hit on the cell that actually contains the letter f in a word.

You can change this setting under Options.

The other way to access Find is through the Editing section of the Home tab. The Find & Select option has a dropdown menu that includes Find.

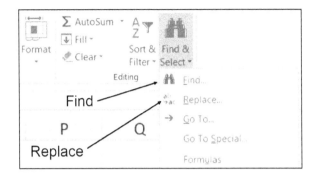

If you're looking for something in order to change it, you can use Replace instead. Type Ctrl and H (Ctrl + H) at the same time (or just Ctrl + F and then click over to the Replace tab), or you can access it through the Editing section of the Home tab.

When the Replace dialogue box opens, you'll see two lines, "Find what" and "Replace with." In the "Find what" line, type what you're looking for. In the "Replace with" line, type what to replace it with.

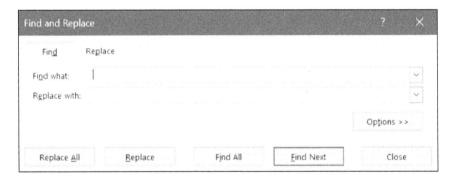

Be VERY careful using Replace. Say you want to replace "hat" with "chapeau" because you've suddenly become pretentious. If you don't think this through, you will end up replacing every usage of hat, even when it's in words like "that" or "chat". So you'll end up with "tchapeau" in the middle of a sentence instead of "that" because the hat portion of that was replaced with chapeau. (This probably happens in Word more than in Excel, but it's still something to be aware of.)

Replace is good for removing something like double spaces or converting formatting of a particular value, but otherwise you might want to use find and then manually correct each entry to avoid inadvertent errors.

Copying Patterns of Data

Sometimes you'll want to input data that repeats itself. Like, for example, the days of the week. Say you're putting together a worksheet that lists the date and what day of the week it is for an entire year. You could type out Monday, Tuesday, Wednesday, Thursday, Friday, Saturday, Sunday, and then copy and paste that 52 times. Or…

You could take advantage of the fact that Excel can recognize patterns. With this particular example, it looks like all it takes is typing in Monday. Do that and then go to the bottom right corner of the cell with Monday in it and position you cursor so that it looks like a small black cross. Left-click, hold that left-click down, and start to drag your cursor away from the cell. Excel should auto-complete the cells below or to the right of the Monday cell with the days of the week in order and repeating themselves in order for as long as you need it to.

If you're dealing with a pattern that isn't as standard as days of the week, sometimes it takes a few rows of data before Excel can identify the pattern. For example, if I type 1 into a cell and try to drag it, Excel just repeats the 1 over and over again. If I do 1 and then 2 and highlight both cells and start to drag from the bottom of the cell with the 2 in it, then it starts to number the next cells 3, 4, 5 etc.

You'll see the values Excel suggests for each cell as you drag the cursor through that cell, but those values won't actually appear in those cells until you're done highlighting all the cells you want to copy the pattern to and you let up on the left-click. (If that doesn't make sense, just try it a few times and you'll see what I mean.)

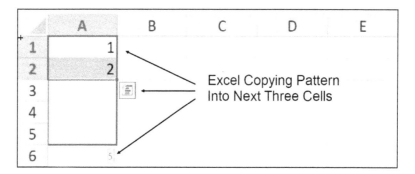

(You can combine Excel's ability to copy patterns with the AutoFill option by double-clicking in the bottom right-hand corner instead. This only works when your current column is next to a column that already has values in it for all of your rows. See the Manipulating Your Data section for more detail on AutoFill.)

Freeze Panes

If you have enough information in a worksheet for it to not be visible in one page, there's a chance you'll want to use freeze panes. What it does is freezes a row or rows and/or a column or columns at the top of your page so that even when you scroll down or to the right those rows or columns stay visible. So if you have 100 rows of information but always want to be able to see your header row, freeze panes will let you do that.

To freeze panes, go to the View tab and click on the arrow under Freeze Panes. It gives you three options: Freeze Panes, Freeze Top Row, and Freeze First Column. Those second two are pretty obvious, right? Choose "Freeze Top Row" and you'll always see Row 1 of your worksheet no matter how far down you scroll. Choose "Freeze First Column" and you'll always see Column A of your worksheet no matter how far to the right you scroll.

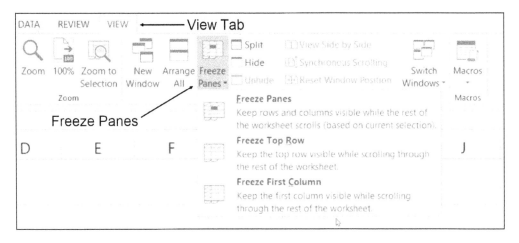

That first option, Freeze Panes, is more interesting. It will freeze as many rows or columns as you need to freeze. If I click on cell C4 (so down three rows and over two columns) and choose to Freeze Panes, it will keep the top three rows and the left two columns of my worksheet visible no matter how far I scroll in the document. So, for example, if you had customer name, city, and state in your first three columns and wanted to be able to see that information as you scrolled over to see other customer data, you could. Or say your worksheet has a couple of rows of text and then the real row labels begin in row 5, you can click in Cell A6, choose to freeze panes, and those top five rows will always stay visible.

Freeze panes is very handy when dealing with large amounts of data. Just be careful that you don't accidentally lose where you are. If you click into a frozen row or column and then arrow down or over, it will take you to the next row, not the data you're seeing on the screen. So if you were looking at row 10,522 and you had the top row frozen and click into row 1 for some reason and then arrow down it will take you to row 2. (It happens to be something I do often, so figured it was worth mentioning.)

To remove freeze panes, you can go back to the View tab and the Freeze Panes dropdown and you'll now see that that first option has become Unfreeze Panes. Just click on it and your document will go back to normal.

FORMATTING

If you're going to spend any amount of time working in Excel then you need to learn how to format cells, because inevitably your column won't be as wide as you want it to be or you'll want to have a cell with red-colored text or to use bolding or italics or something that isn't Excel's default.

That's what this section is for. It's an alphabetical listing of different things you might want to do. You can either format one cell at a time by highlighting that specific cell, or you can format multiple cells at once by highlighting all of them and then choosing your formatting option.

What you'll see below is that there are basically two main ways to format cells. You can use the Home tab and click on the option you want from there, or you can right-click and select the Format Cells option from the dropdown menu. For basic formatting, the Home tab will be the best choice. For less common formatting choices, you may need to use the Format Cells option.

There are also shortcut keys available for things like bolding (Ctrl + B), italicizing (Ctrl + I), and underlining (Ctrl +U) that give a third option for some basic formatting needs.

Aligning Your Text Within a Cell

By default, text within a cell is left-aligned and bottom-aligned. But at times you may want to adjust this. I often will center text or prefer for it to be top-aligned because it looks better to me that way when I have some column headers that are one line and others that are multiple lines.

To do this, highlight the cell(s) you want to change, and go to the Alignment section on the Home tab. You'll see on the left-hand side of that section six different images with lines in them. These are visual representations of your possible choices. The first row has the top aligned, middle aligned, and bottom aligned options. You can choose one of these three options for your cell. The second row has the left-aligned, centered, and right-aligned options. You can also choose one of these three options for your cell. So you can have a cell with top-aligned and centered text or top-aligned and right-aligned text or bottom-aligned and centered text, etc.

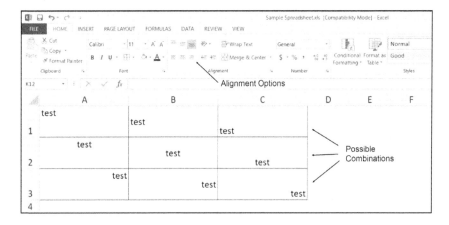

The angled "ab" with an arrow under it on the top row of the Alignment section also has a handful of pre-defined options for changing the direction of text within a cell. You can choose to Angle Counterclockwise, Angle Clockwise, Vertical Text, Rotate Text Up, and Rotate Text Down. (It also offers another way to access the Alignment tab of the Format Cells dialogue box which we'll talk about next. Just click on Format Cell Alignment at the bottom of the dropdown menu.)

Another way to change the text alignment within a cell(s) is to highlight your cell(s) and then right-click and choose Format Cells from the dropdown menu.

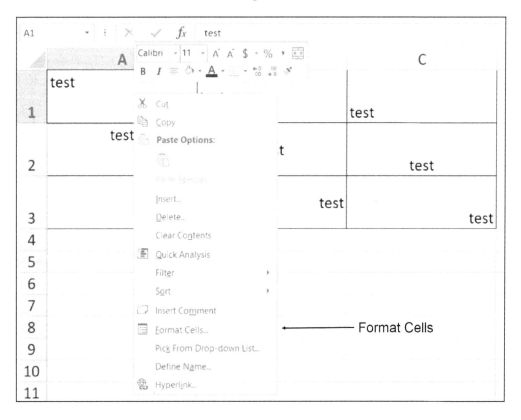

When the Format Cells dialogue box opens, go to the Alignment tab.

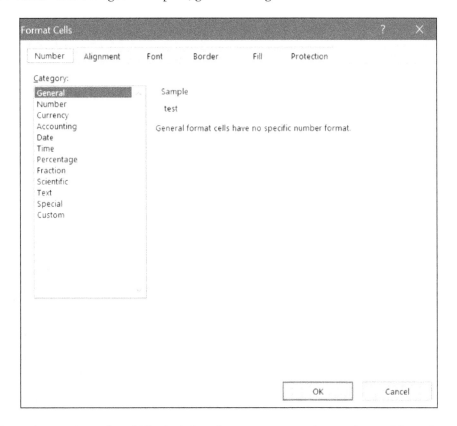

Choose from the Horizontal and Vertical dropdown menus to change the position of text within a cell (Top, Center, Bottom, Left, Right, etc.).

The Horizontal and Vertical dropdown menus have a few additional choices (like Justify and Distributed), but you generally shouldn't need them. (And be wary of Fill which it seems will repeat whatever you have in that cell over and over again until it fills the cell. Remember, if you do something you don't like, Ctrl + Z.)

You can also change the orientation of your text so that it's vertical or angled by entering the number of degrees (90 to make it vertical) or moving the line within the Orientation box to where you want it.

Bolding Text

You can bold text in a number of ways.

First, you can highlight the cell(s) you want bolded and click on the large capital B in the Font section of the Home tab.

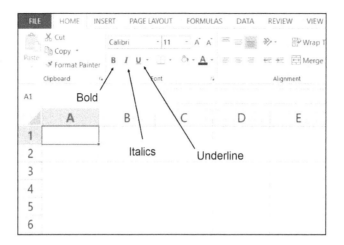

Second, you can highlight the cell(s) you want bolded and then type Ctrl and B at the same time. (Ctrl + B)

Or, third, you can highlight the cell(s) you want to bold and then right-click and choose Format Cells from the dropdown menu. Once you're in the Format Cells dialogue box, go to the Font tab and choose Bold from the Font Style options. If you want text that is both bolded and italicized, choose Bold Italic.

You can also bold just part of the text in a cell by clicking into the cell, highlighting the portion of the text that you want to bold, and then using any of the above methods.

To remove bolding from text or cells that already have it, highlight the bolded portion and then type Ctrl + B or click on the large capital B in the Font section of the Home tab. (If you happen to highlight text that is only partially bolded you may have to do it twice to remove the bold formatting.)

Borders Around Cells

It's nice to have borders around your data to keep the information in each cell distinct, especially if you're going to print your document.

There are two main ways to add borders around a cell or set of cells. First, you can highlight the cells you want to place a border around and then go to the Font section on the Home tab and choose from the Borders dropdown option. It's a four-square grid with an arrow next to it that's located between the U used for underlining and the color bucket used for filling a cell with color. Click on the arrow to see your available options, and then choose the type of border you want. (If you just want a simple border all around the cells and between multiple cells click on the All Borders option.)

With this option, to adjust the line thickness or line colors, see the options in the Draw Borders section, but be sure to choose your colors and line style before you choose your border type because the color and line type you choose will only apply to borders you draw after you choose them.

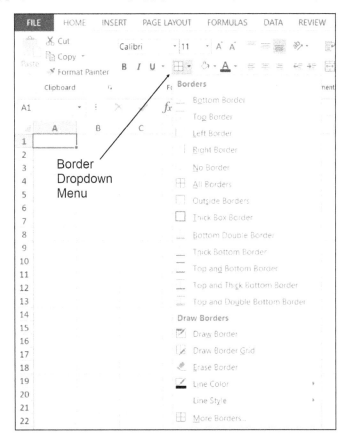

You can combine border types to get the appearance you want. For example, you could choose All Borders for the entire set of cells and then Thick Box Border to put a darker outline around the perimeter.

Your second choice is to highlight the cells where you want to place a border and then right-click and select Format Cells from the dropdown menu. Next, go to the Border tab and choose your border style, type, and color from there.

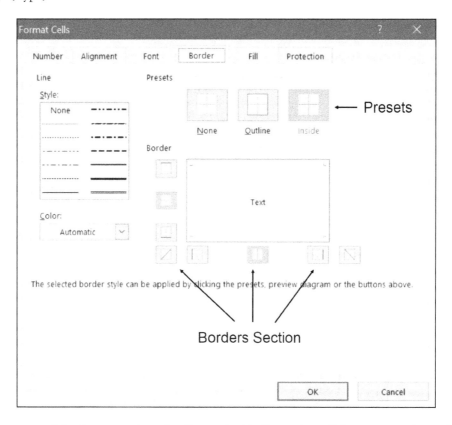

If you want one of the Preset options (outline or inside lines), just click on it. To clear what you've done and start over you can select None from the Presets section.

If you want only a subset of lines (for example, only the bottom of the cell to have a line), click on the choice you want from the Border section around the Text box. You can click on more than one of the lines in this section. So you could have, for example, a top and bottom border, but nothing else.

And, if you want to change the style of a line or its color from the default, you should do so in the Line section before you select where you want your lines to appear.

You can see what you've chosen and what it will look like in the sample box in the center of the screen.

Coloring a Cell (Fill Color)

You can color (or fill) an entire cell with almost any color you want. To do this, highlight the cell(s) you want to color, go to the Font section of the Home tab, and click on the arrow to the right of the paint bucket that has a yellow line under it. This should bring up a colors menu with 70 difference colors to choose from, including many that are arranged as complementary themes. If you want one of those colors, just click on it.

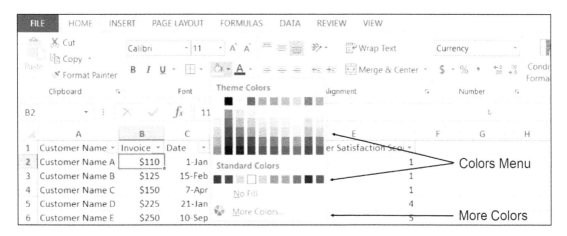

If none of those colors work for you, or you need to use a specific corporate color, click on More Colors at the bottom. This will bring up a Colors display box. The first tab of that box looks like a honeycomb and has a number of colors you can choose from by clicking into the honeycomb. The second tab is the Custom tab. It has a rainbow of colors that you can click on and also allows you to enter specific red, green, and blue values to get the exact color you need. (If you have a corporate color palette, they should give you the RGB values for each of the colors. At least my last employer did.)

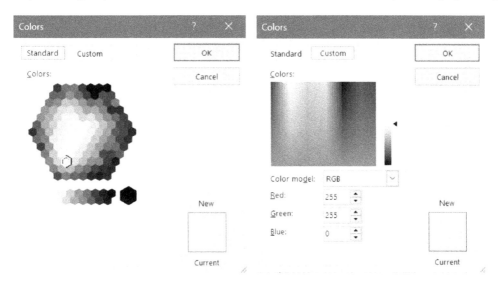

On the Custom tab, you can also use the arrow on the right-hand side to darken or lighten your color. With both tabs, you can see the color you've chosen in the bottom right corner. If you like your choice, click on OK. If you don't want to add color to a cell after all, choose Cancel.

Column Width (Adjusting)

If your columns aren't the width you want, you have three options for adjusting them.

First, you can right-click on the column and choose Column Width from the dropdown menu. When the box showing you the current column width appears, enter a new column width.

Second, you can place your cursor to the right side of the column name—it should look like a line with arrows on either side—and then left-click and hold while you move the cursor to the right or the left until the column is as wide as you want it to be.

Or, third, you can place your cursor on the right side of the column name and double left-click. This will make the column as wide or as narrow as the widest text currently in that column. (Usually. Sometimes this one has a mind of its own.)

To adjust all column widths in your document at once, you can highlight the entire worksheet and then double-left click on any column border and it will adjust each column to the contents in that column. (Usually. See comment above.)

To have uniform column widths throughout your worksheet, highlight the whole worksheet, right-click on a column, choose Column Width, and set your column width. Highlighting the whole worksheet and then left-clicking and dragging one column to the desired width will also work.

Currency Formatting

If you type a number into a cell in Excel, it'll just show that number. So, 25 is 25. $25 is $25. But sometimes you want those numbers to display as currency with the dollar sign and cents showing, too. Or you've already copied in unformatted numbers and now want them to have the same currency format.

To do this, highlight the cell(s) you want formatted this way, and then go to the Number section of the Home tab, and click on the $ sign.

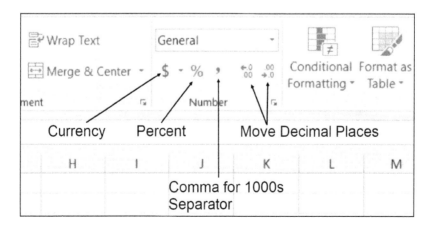

Another option is to highlight the cells you want formatted that way, go to the Number section of the Home tab, and use the dropdown to choose either Currency or Accounting.

You can also highlight the cell(s), right-click, choose the Format Cells option, go to the Number tab, and choose either Currency or Accounting from there.

Date Formatting

Sometimes Excel has a mind of its own about how to format dates. For example, if I type in 1/1 for January 1st, Excel will show it as 1-Jan. It means the same thing, but if I would rather it display as 1/1/2017, I need to change the formatting.

To do this, click on the cell with your date in it, go to the Number section on the Home tab, click on the dropdown menu, and choose Short Date. (You can also choose Long Date if you prefer that format.)

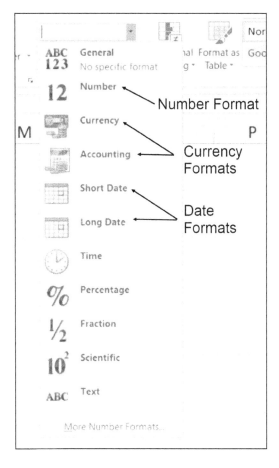

Another option is to highlight your cell(s), right click, choose Format Cells from the dropdown menu, go to the Number tab of the Format Cells dialogue box, and choose your date format from there by clicking on Date and then selecting one of the numerous choices it provides.

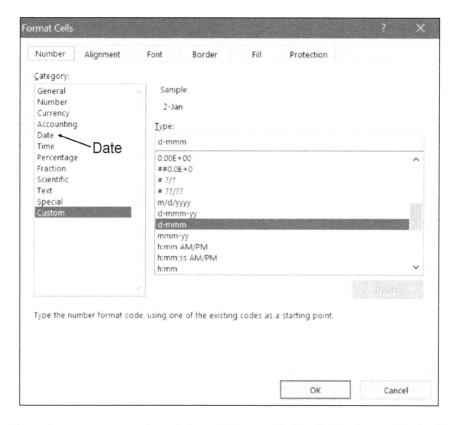

Note that if you just enter a month and day of the month like I did above, Excel will default to assuming that you meant the date to be for the current year and will store your date as MM-DD-YYYY even if you weren't trying to specify a year.

Font Choice and Size

In my version of Excel the default font choice is Calibri and the default font size is 11 point. You may have strong preferences about what font you use or work for a company that uses specific fonts for its brand or just want some variety in terms of font size or type within a specific document. In that case, you will need to change your font.

There are two ways to do this.

First, you can highlight the cells you want to change or the specific text you want to change, and go to the Font section on the Home tab. Select a different font or font size from the dropdown menus there.

You also have the option to increase or decrease the font one size at a time by clicking on the A's with little arrows in the top right corner that are next to the font dropdown box.

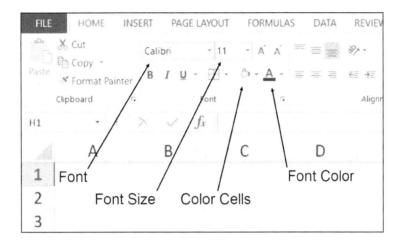

Second, you can highlight the cells or text you want to change, right-click, and choose Format Cells from the dropdown menu, and then go to the Font tab and choose your Font and Size from the listed values.

With either option, you can choose a font size that isn't listed by clicking into the font size box and typing the value you want.

Font Color

The default color for all text in Excel is black, but you can change that if you want or need to. (For example, if you've colored a cell with a darker color you may want to consider changing the font color to white to make the text in that cell more visible.)

You have two options. First, you can highlight the cells or the specific text you want to change, go to the Font section on the Home tab, and click on the arrow next to the A with a red line under it (see image above). You can then choose from one of the 70 colors that are listed, and if those aren't enough of a choice you can click on More Colors and select your color from the Colors dialogue box. (See Coloring a Cell for more detail about that option.)

Second, you can highlight the cell or text, right-click and choose Format Cells from the drop-down menu, go to the Font tab, and then click on the dropdown menu under Color which will bring up the same seventy color options and the ability to choose More Colors and add a custom color instead.

Italicizing Text

You do this by highlighting the cell(s) you want italicized and clicking on the slanted I in the Font section on the Home tab (see image under the Bolding description), or by highlighting the cell(s) and holding down the Ctrl key and the I key at the same time. (Ctrl + I)

Or, you can highlight the cell(s), right-click, choose Format Cells from the dropdown menu, go to the Font tab, and choose Italic from the Font Style options. (See image under the Bolding description.)

You can also italicize just part of the text in a cell by only selecting that portion and then using one of the methods above.

To remove italics from text or cells that already have it, you follow the exact same steps. (Highlight your selection and then type Ctrl + I or click on the slanted I in the Font section on the Home tab.)

Merge & Center

Merge and Center is a specialized command that can come in handy when you're working with a table where you want a header that spans multiple columns of data. (Don't use it if you plan to do a lot of data analysis with what you've input into the worksheet because it will mess with your ability to filter, sort, or use pivot tables. It's really for creating a finalized, pretty-looking report.)

If you're going to merge and center text, make sure that the text you want to keep is in the top-most and left-most of the cells you plan to merge and center. Data in the other cells that are being merged will be deleted. (You'll get a warning message to this effect if you have values in any of the other cells.)

You can merge cells across columns and down rows. So you could, for example, merge four cells that span two columns and two rows into one big cell while keeping all of the other cells in those columns and rows separate.

Highlight all of the cells you want to merge. Next, go to the Alignment section of the Home tab and choose Merge & Center. This will combine your selected cells into one cell and center the contents from the topmost, left-most cell that was merged across the selection.

You'll see on that dropdown that you can also choose to just Merge Across (which will just merge the cells in the first row) or to Merge Cells (which will merge the cells but won't center the text).

Also, if you ever need to unmerge those merged cells you can do so by selecting the Unmerge Cells option from that dropdown.

You can also Merge Cells by highlighting the cells, right-clicking, selecting the Format Cells option, going to the Alignment tab, and then choosing to Merge Cells from there. If you choose that option, you have to center the text separately.

Number Formatting

Sometimes when you copy data into Excel it doesn't format it the way you want. For example, I have a report I receive that includes ISBN numbers which are 10- or 13- digit numbers. When I copy those into Excel, it sometimes displays them in Scientific Number format (9.78E+12) as opposed to as a normal number.

To change the formatting of your data to a number format, you have two options.

First, you can highlight the cell(s) and go to the Number section of the Home tab. From the drop-down menu choose Number. (Sometimes General will work as well.) It will then convert it to a number with two decimal places. So 100.00 instead of 100. You can then use the zeroes with arrows next to them that are below the drop-down box to adjust how many decimal places display. The one with the right-pointing arrow will reduce the number of decimal places. The one with the left-pointing arrow will increase them. (See the Currency Formatting section for an image.)

Second, you can highlight the cell(s), right-click, select Format Cells from the dropdown, go to the Number tab, choose Number on the left-hand side listing, and then in the middle, choose your number of decimal places. You can also choose whether to use a comma to separate out your thousands and millions and how to display negative numbers at the same time.

Percent Formatting

To format numbers as a percentage, highlight the cell(s), and click on the percent sign in the Number section of the Home tab.

You can also highlight the cell(s), right-click, select Format Cells from the dropdown, go to the Number tab, choose Percentage on the left-hand side, and then in the middle, choose your number of decimal places.

Row Height (Adjusting)

If your rows aren't the correct height, you have three options for adjusting them. First, you can right-click on the row you want to adjust, choose Row Height from the dropdown menu, and when the box showing you the current row height appears, enter a new row height.

Second, you can place your cursor along the lower border of the row number until it looks like a line with arrows above and below. Left-click and hold while you move the cursor up or down until the row is as tall as you want it to be.

Third, you can place your cursor along the lower border of the row, and double left-click. This will fit the row height to the text in the cell. (Usually.)

To adjust all row heights in your document at once you can highlight the entire worksheet and then double-left click on any row border and it will adjust each row to the contents in each individual row. (Usually.) To have uniform row heights throughout your worksheet, you can highlight the whole sheet, right-click on a row, choose Row Height and set your row height that way or select the entire worksheet, right-click on the border below a row, and adjust that row to the height you want for all rows.

Underlining Text

You have three options for underlining text. First, you can highlight the cell(s) you want underlined and click on the underlined U in the Font section on the Home tab. (See the Bolding section for a screen shot.)

Second, you can highlight the cell(s) and type Ctrl and U at the same time. (Ctrl + U)

Third, you can highlight the cell(s), right-click, choose Format Cells from the dropdown menu, go to the Font tab, and choose the type of underlining you want (single, double, single accounting, double accounting) from the Underline drop down menu.

You can also underline part of the text in a cell by clicking into the cell, highlighting the portion of the text that you want to underline, and then using any of the above methods.

To remove underlining from text or cells that already have it, highlight the text and then use one of the above options.

Wrapping Text

Sometimes you want to read all of the text in a cell, but you don't want that column to be wide enough to display all of the text. This is where the Wrap Text option becomes useful, because it will keep your text within the width of the column and display it on multiple lines by "wrapping" the text.

(Excel does have a limit as to how many rows of text it will display in one cell, so if you have any cells with lots of text in them, check to make sure that the full contents of the cell are actually visible. You may have to manually adjust the row height to see all of the text.)

To Wrap Text in a cell, select the cell(s), go to the Alignment section of the Home Tab, and click on the Wrap Text option in the Alignment section.

Or you can highlight the cell(s), right-click, choose Format Cells from the dropdown menu, go to the Alignment tab there, and choose Wrap Text under Text Control.

* * *

One final formatting trick to share with you that is incredibly handy. (Maybe more so in Word than in Excel, but I use it frequently in both.)

Copying Formatting From One Cell To Another

In addition to the specific formatting options discussed above, if you already have a cell formatted the way you want it to, you can "Format Sweep" from that cell to other cells you want formatted the same way. You do this by using the Format Painter in the Clipboard section of the Home tab.

Highlight the cell(s) that have the formatting you want to copy (if the formatting is identical, just highlight one cell), click on the Format Painter, and then click into the cell(s) you want to copy the formatting to. The contents in the destination cell will remain the same, but the font, font color, font size, cell borders, italics/bolding/underlining, and text alignment and orientation will all change to match that of the cell that you swept the formatting from.

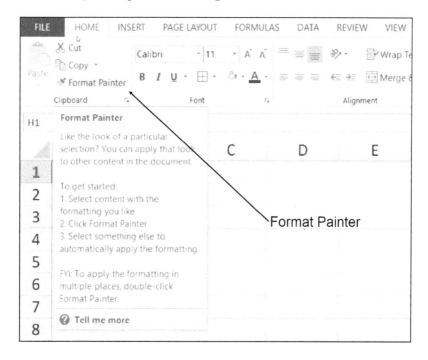

You need to be careful using the format sweeper because it will change *all* formatting in your destination cells. So, if the cell you're copying the formatting from is bolded and has red text, both of those attributes will copy over even if all you were trying to do was copy the bold formatting. (This is more of a problem when using the tool in Word than in Excel, but it's still something to watch out for especially if you have borders around cells.)

Also, the tool copies formatting to whatever cell you select next, which can be a problem if the cell you're copying from isn't next to the one you're copying to. Do not use arrow keys to navigate between the cells. You need to click directly from the cell with the formatting you want to the cell you're transferring the formatting to.

(Remember, Ctrl + Z is your friend if you make a mistake.)

If you have more than one isolated cell that you need to apply formatting to, you can double-click the Format Painter and it will continue to copy the formatting of the original cell to every other cell you click in until you click on the Format Painter again or hit Esc. (You'll know the tool is still in operation because there will be a little broom next to your cursor.)

You can copy formatting from multiple cells to multiple cells, so say the formatting for an entire row to an entire other row, but be sure to double-check the results since this is much more likely to result in unintended formatting.

Also, you can copy formatting from one cell to multiple cells at a time by simply highlighting all of the cells you want to copy the formatting to at once.

If you format sweep and then undo, you'll see that the cell(s) you were trying to format from are surrounded by a dotted border as if you had copied the cells. Be sure to hit the Esc key before you continue.

MANIPULATING YOUR DATA

Once you've entered your data into a worksheet, you might want to do something with it. Like sort it or filter it so you see only the entries that meet specific criteria, or analyze it using mathematical functions like addition or subtraction. This section will walk you through the basics of sorting, filtering, and analyzing your data.

Sorting

Sorting allows you to display your information in a specific order. For example, by date, value, or alphabetically. You can also sort across multiple columns, so you can, for example, sort first by date, then by name, then by amount.

To sort your data, select all cells that contain your information, including your header row if there is one.

If you set your data up with the first row as the header and all of the rest as data, you can just click in the top left corner of your worksheet to select all of the cells in the worksheet. Excel will then figure out the limits of your data when you choose to sort.

If you have a table of data that starts lower down on the page or that has a summary row or that is followed by other data, be sure to only select the cells in the data set you want to sort, because Excel will sort everything you select whether it makes sense to do so or not.

Once you've selected your data, go to the Editing section of the Home tab. Click on the arrow next to Sort & Filter, and choose Custom Sort. Your other option is to go to the Data tab and click on the Sort option there. Either path will bring you to the Sort dialogue box.

The first choice you need to make is to indicate whether or not your data has headers. In other words, does the first row of your data contain column labels? If so, click on that box in the top corner that says, "My data has headers." If you indicate that there is a header row, it will not be included in your sort and will remain the first row of your data.

When you do this, you'll see that your Sort By dropdown now displays your column labels. If you don't check this box, the dropdown will show generic column names (Column A, Column B, etc.) and all of your data will be sorted, including the first row.

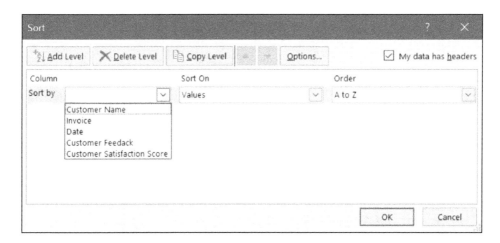

Sometimes Excel tries to decide this for you and is wrong, so always make sure that your Sort By choices make sense given the data you selected, and that you check or uncheck the "My data has headers" box to get the result you want.

The next step is to choose your sort order.

What is the first criteria you want to sort by? Chose that column from the Sort By dropdown menu.

Next, choose *how* to sort that column of data. You can sort on values, font color, cell color, and icon. I almost always use values.

After that, choose what order to use. For text it's usually from A to Z to sort alphabetical or from Z to A to sort reverse alphabetical. I also sometimes use the Custom List option when I have a column with the months of the year or the days of the week in it. For numbers it's just Smallest to Largest or Largest to Smallest.

If all you want to sort by is one column, then you're done. Click OK.

If you want to sort first by the column you already entered and then by another column, you need to add the second column. Click on Add Level and select your next column to sort by and your criteria for that sort.

If you add a level you don't need, highlight it and choose Delete Level.

If you have multiple levels but decide that they should be sorted in a different order, you can use the arrows to the left of Options to move a sort level up or down.

The default is to sort top to bottom, but you can click on Options to sort left to right or to make your sort case sensitive.

When you're done with your sort options, click OK. If you change your mind, click Cancel. If you get a sort that has a mistake in it, remember to use Ctrl + Z to undo and try again.

A few things to watch out for with sort order. Be sure that you've selected all of the data you want sorted. If you only highlight three columns but have six columns of data, only the first three columns will be sorted. The other three columns will stay in their original order which will break the relationship between your data points.

Excel also offers quick-sort options (the ones that say Sort A to Z or Sort Z to A), but be wary when using them. Sometimes they work great, most times they sort in the wrong order for me or on the wrong column or miss that I have a header row. To save myself time and effort, I usually just use Custom Sort instead.

Filtering

Sometimes you want your data to stay right where it is, but you want to see only certain results that meet a specific criteria. For example, only customers located in Mozambique. Filtering allows you to do that. As long as your data is displayed in rows (and ideally with contiguous columns), you can use filtering.

To start, click on any cell in the header row of your data, and then in the Editing section of the Home tab, click on the arrow next to Sort & Filter and choose Filter.

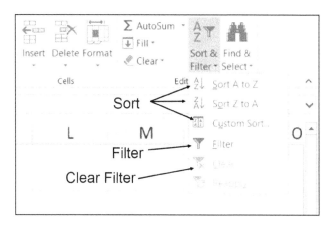

You should now see gray arrows to the right of each label in your first row.

One thing to note here is that the Filter function will only show arrows for columns that are touching. So if you have data in Columns A through D and then in Columns F through K, it will show the filter arrows for either Columns A through D OR Columns F through K, but not for both sets of columns at the same time. If you want to be able to filter on all of those columns at once, you need to remove any blank columns in between.

What I'm about to discuss applies to more recent versions of Excel, but not older versions. As I recall, older versions basically let you filter on one column and with limited criteria. You certainly couldn't filter by color until very recently. So if you have an older version of Excel you may be able to filter your results some, but not as well as with more recent versions. And if you save into an older version of Excel while your data is filtered, you may experience issues with how your data displays. If I recall correctly it keeps the filtering you had in place, but doesn't show all of the filtering choices you made. (I usually don't keep filters on my data. I use filtering to view my data while I'm working, but then I remove them before I close the file.)

Okay. Back to how to filter.

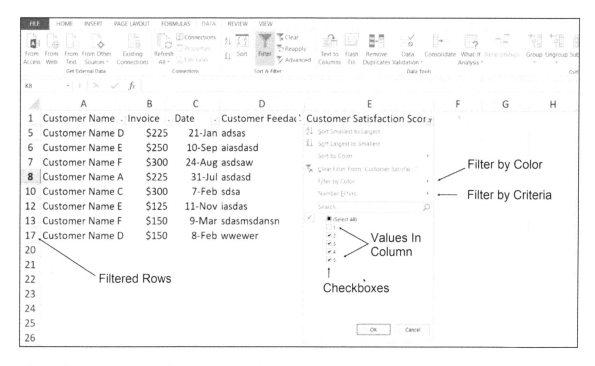

If you click on the arrow for any given column, you should see a list of all potential values in that column with checkboxes next to each value. For really long data sets (tens of thousands of rows) this may not be a complete listing. It definitely wasn't in older versions of Excel.

For basic filtering, you can use the checkboxes to set the criteria for what data to display. Simply uncheck the box for any values you don't want to see.

Or, if you want to see only one or two of the values, what you can do is click in the Select All box to unselect all of the values, and then click in the box for the one or two you want to see.

You can also type the name of the value you want to filter by into the Search field.

Or you can filter by criteria instead. Depending on the type of data you're filtering, the option will say Number Filters or Text Filters.

Click on the arrow and you should see options like "Equals" or "Does Not Equal" or "Begins With" or "Between" etc. The options differ depending on whether it's text or a number. You can use these filter criteria to select only the rows where those criteria are met. So, for example, you can filter to include only invoices over $500 or only customers in Canada.

Or, invoices over $500 for customers in Canada. Current versions of Excel allow you to filter on multiple columns at once.

If you've color-coded cells using Font color or Cell color, you can also filter by those criteria, using the Filter by Color option.

When cells in your worksheet are filtered, the row numbers in your worksheet will be colored blue, and you'll see that the row numbers skip since some rows won't be displayed. (In the screenshot above, rows 2, 3, 4, 9, 11, 14, 15, and 16 have been filtered out because they had customer satisfaction scores of 1.)

Columns where filtering is in place will show a funnel instead of an arrow on the gray dropdown next to the column name.

To remove filtering from a specific column, click on the gray arrow, and select Clear Filter from [Column Name].

To remove all filtering in a worksheet, go to the Editing section of the Home tab, click on Sort & Filter, and then choose Clear.

* * *

Alright, that was sorting and filtering. Let's talk functions now.

For any function, start with an equals sign (=) in the cell. That tells Excel that you're calculating something in this cell and to look for a function or mathematical symbol (like a * for multiplication).

Excel has hundreds of functions but the ones you'll probably use the most are the basic math functions, so we'll start there.

Basic Math Functions

Basic math functions in my definition are addition, subtraction, multiplication, and division. The below image shows simple formulas for each of the four basic math functions. The first column is when two values are involved, the second column is for when multiple values are involved. We'll walk through each one in a second, but note that for addition and multiplication there are named functions that you can use (SUM and PRODUCT, respectively) when multiple values are involved, but there are no named functions for subtraction or division.

While all of the examples I'm about to use focus on data in one worksheet, you can perform functions across worksheets. It's the same process, just click on the cell you want to use in the worksheet where it's located and Excel will take care of the rest.

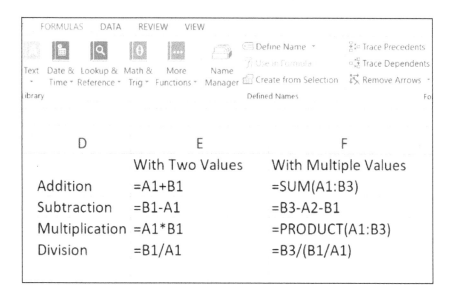

D	With Two Values	With Multiple Values
Addition	=A1+B1	=SUM(A1:B3)
Subtraction	=B1-A1	=B3-A2-B1
Multiplication	=A1*B1	=PRODUCT(A1:B3)
Division	=B1/A1	=B3/(B1/A1)

Alright, let's walk through each one in more detail.

Addition

If you just want to know what the value of some cells added together is, but you don't need it recorded in your worksheet, you actually don't even need to use a function. You can just highlight the cells you want to add together and then look in the bottom right corner of the worksheet. It should show you the average, the count, and the sum of the cells you have highlighted.

But if you want the results of that addition visible in a cell in the worksheet, then you need to use either the + sign or the SUM( ) function.

The + sign tells Excel to add the two values on each side of the sign together. So above where it says =A1+B1 that's telling Excel to add the values in cell A1 and cell B1. You can also write it as =25+35 and have Excel add 25 to 35. You don't have to use cell references, but remember that normally in Excel all you'll see displayed is the result of a calculation. The only way to know what values were combined is to click on the specific cell and look in the formula bar.

If you have more than one value to add together, you can use the SUM function. The easiest way to do this is to type

=SUM(

into your cell and then highlight the cells you want to add together. Excel will convert the cells you've highlighted into the proper notation.

As you can see above, the formula for the example is =SUM(A1:B3). This is adding cells A1, B1, A2, B2, A3, and B3 together. Rather than try to figure out the proper way to summarize that, it's best to let Excel do it. But if you want to do it yourself, basically a colon between cells (:) means "through" and a comma (,) means "and." So =SUM(A1,B3) would mean add A1 to B3.

Also, to reference an entire column leave out the row references. So =SUM(B:B) means sum all of the values in column B. And =SUM(B:C) means sum all of the values in columns B and C.

If you want to make sure that you entered your formula correctly, note that when you type a formula into Excel it will highlight the cells included in the formula.

To check the contents of a formula later, double-click on the cell with the formula and Excel will highlight the cells being used, and will color-code them as well. (Very helpful with nested IF functions, which are covered in the *Intermediate Excel* guide.)

With addition, you also have one other option. You can use the AutoSum option in the Editing section of the Home Tab. This is basically just another way to create your formula for you.

The AutoSum icon looks like the mathematical sum function (a big pointy E-like shape). Click in the cell either below or to the right of the numbers you want to add together, click on AutoSum, and Excel will highlight all contiguous numbers either above the cell or to the left of it, and create a SUM formula for you using those cells. The AutoSum option stops at blank lines, so if you need to sum across a blank space, you'll need to edit the formula for it to work.

Subtraction

There are no nifty shortcuts when it comes to subtraction. You basically just have to type in a formula using the negative sign. The basic format is =( )–( )–( ) where the parens represent your different values. So if I want to subtract the value in cell B1 from the value in cell A1 I would type =A1-B1.

If I want to subtract B1, C1, and D1 from A1 I could either type =A1-B1-C1-D1 or I could also use the SUM function and type =A1-SUM(B1:D1) since that gets the same result.

As with any type of subtraction, be sure you get the numbers in the right order. The number you're starting with goes on the left-hand side, the number you're taking away from that goes on the right-hand side.

Also, you can still click on the cells you need instead of typing the whole formula. So, start with =, click on the first cell you need, type - , and click on the next one. Not as useful for subtraction as it is for addition, because you can't really use it with multiple cells at once.

Multiplication

Multiplication basically works the same way as addition. You can use the function PRODUCT or you can use the star symbol (*) between two values you want to multiply together.

So if you want to multiply cell A1 by cell B1, you'd type =A1*B1 or =PRODUCT (A1:B1) or =PRODUCT (A1, B1). All three formulas will get you the same result.

For multiple values, it would be =A1*B1*C1 or =PRODUCT (A1:C1) or =PRODUCT(A1,B1,C1).

Division

Division, much like subtraction, is another one where order matters. In the case of division you use the right slash (/) to indicate that the number on the left-hand side should be divided by the number on the right-hand side.

So if I want to divide A1 by B1, I would type =A1/B1.

It's best not to divide multiple numbers in one cell, because it's prone to error and it's better to see your steps as you go, but if you do so, make sure to use parens to ensure that the correct numbers get divided since =(A1/B1)/C1 is different than =A1/(B1/C1).

Complex Formulas

As I just hinted, you can definitely do much more complex formulas in Excel. You just have to make sure you write it properly so that Excel knows which functions to perform first.

Put something in parens and Excel will do that before anything else. Otherwise it will follow standard mathematical principles about which actions to perform in which order.

According to the Excel help documentation (under Operator Precedence), Excel will first combine cells (B1:B3 or B1, B2), then create any negative numbers (-B1), then create percents, then calculate any exponentials (B2^2), then do any multiplication and division, then do any addition and subtraction, then concatenate any values, and then do any comparisons last.

All of this, of course, at least in the U.S., is done from left to right in a formula.

So, basically, Excel calculates starting on the left side of the equation and moves to the right, doing each of those steps above in that order throughout the entire formula before circling back to the start and doing the next step. Which means that multiplication and division are done first and then addition or subtraction.

Of course, anything in parens is treated as a standalone equation first. So if you have =3*(4+2), Excel will add the 4 and the 2 before it does the multiplication.

Basically, if you're going to write complex formulas they're definitely doable but you should be very comfortable with math and how it works. Also, be sure to test your equation to make sure you did it right. I do this by breaking a formula into its component steps and then making sure that my combined equation generates the same result.

Other Functions

Excel has a ton of available functions that can do all sorts of interesting things and not just with numbers.

To see what I'm talking about, go to the Formulas tab. There are seven different subject areas listed there (Financial, Logical, Text, Date & Time, Lookup & Reference, Math & Trig, and Other). Click on each of those dropdowns and you'll see twenty-plus functions for each one.

But how do you know if there's a function that does what you want to do? For example, is there a function for trimming excess space from a string of values? (Yes. It's called TRIM.) Or for calculating the cumulative principal paid on a loan between two periods? (Yes.)

So how do you find the function you want without hovering over each function to see what it does?

The simple way is to go to the Formulas tab and click on Insert Function. This will bring up the Insert Function dialogue box which includes a search function. Type a few words for what you're looking for.

For example, if I want to calculate how many days until some event occurs and I want to have this formula work no matter what day it is when I open my worksheet, then I need some way to set a value equal to today's date whatever day today is. So I search for "today" and get a function called TODAY that it says "Returns the current date formatted as a date." Perfect.

Or what if I have two columns of text and I want to combine them. If I search for "combine text" my second option is CONCATENATE which is described as "Joins several text strings into one text string." That'll work.

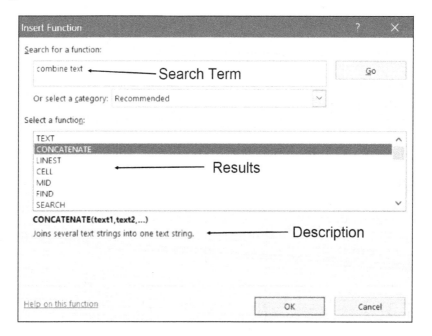

Once you've found a function you like, highlight it and click on OK. Excel will take you back to the worksheet and show you a Function Arguments dialogue box that tells you what inputs are needed to create that particular function.

So for CONCATENATE it shows me boxes for Text 1 and Text 2, because to write a concatenate function you need to at least write =CONCATENATE(A1, B1) where A1 and B1 are the two cells you're combining.

Sometimes selecting a function this way, even if you know what it does, is helpful because it shows you what order you need to put the information in and what form it needs to take. But you can also see this to a lesser degree when you start to type the function into your cell. Once you type the opening paren it will show you the components you need and their order. (Very helpful for things like SUMIF and SUMIFS that have different orders even though they do similar things.)

As a side note, TRIM, CONCATENATE, and SUMIFS are all discussed in further detail in *Intermediate Excel*.

Copying Cells With Formulas in Them

One of the nice things about working with formulas in Excel is that you don't have to type them over and over and over again. You can type a formula once and if you need to use it again, simply copy it to a new cell.

There are some tricks to copying formulas. So let's walk through those.

By default, formulas are relative. Meaning that if you have a formula that says =B1+C1 and you copy it (Ctrl + C) over to the right one cell it will become =C1+D1. If you copy it down one cell from that original location it will become =B2+C2. This is great when you have rows and rows of data with everything located in the same position and want to perform the exact same calculation on each of those rows. You can simply copy the formula and paste it down the entire column and it will perform that calculation on each and every row.

But sometimes you just want to move the calculation. Say it's in Cell B2 now and you want to put it in Cell A10. That's when you need to cut the formula (Ctrl + X) and move it instead of copy it. By cutting and moving the formula, it stays the exact same. If it said =B1+C1 it still does.

Another way to do this is to click into the cell, highlight all of the text in the cell, copy it, and tab (or Esc) out of the cell, and then click on the new location and paste it. (If you click into the cell, highlight all of the text, and try to click on where you want to paste it, you'll end up replacing your existing text in the source cell with a reference to the cell you clicked into.)

What if you want to copy the formula, but you want to keep some portion of it fixed. Either the row reference, the column reference, or the reference to an entire cell. (Useful when calculating different scenarios where you build a table with different values for variable x in one row and different values for variable y in one column and then calculate what value you get for each combination of x and y. So, hourly pay and hours worked, for example.)

You can fix a portion of a formula by using the $ sign. (We discussed it earlier with respect to inputting data, but I'll run through it again here.)

To fix the reference to a cell, put a $ sign before both the letter and the number in the cell name. So cell B2 becomes B2 in your formula. If you reference a cell that way (B2), no matter where you copy that formula to it will continue to reference that specific cell. This is useful if you have a constant listed somewhere that's used in a calculation performed for a number of rows. So say you're selling widgets and they're all priced at $100. You might list Widget Price at the top of your worksheet and put 100 in a cell at the top and then calculate how much each customer owes by multiplying their units purchased by that fixed value.

If you want to keep just the column the same, but change the row reference, put the dollar sign in front of the letter only. So $B2 when copied would become $B3, $B4, etc.

If you want to keep the row the same, but change the column reference, you'd put the dollar sign in front of the number only. So B$2. When copied, that portion of the formula would change to C$2, D$2, etc.

One more thought about copying formulas. I usually just highlight all of the cells where I want to copy the formula to and then paste, but there's a shortcut that you can sometimes use that's faster when you have many many rows of data.

If you have a formula in a cell and want to copy it downward and the column where that cell is located is touching another column of data that has already been completed (so you have a full column of data next to the column where you want to put your formula), you can place your cursor on the bottom right corner of the cell with the formula and double-left click. This should copy the formula down all of your rows of data.

It doesn't work if the other column of data hasn't been filled in yet. Excel only knows how far to copy the formula based on the information in the other column. But it can be a handy shortcut in a table with lots of completed information where you're just adding a calculation.

Select All

Another little trick that comes in handy when I'm working with data I've already added to my worksheet is the ability to select all of the contents of the worksheet at once. To do this, click on the top left corner of the sheet where the rows and columns meet. In this version of Excel the bottom half of the square is light gray.

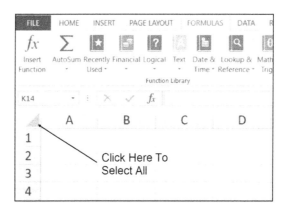

Doing this will select all of the rows and columns in the worksheet and allow you to easily copy the contents so you can move them to another worksheet. Usually I do this when I want to use the Paste Special – Values option to remove any formulas from the worksheet. I Select All, Copy, Paste Special-Values and that overwrites the entire worksheet with just that values that were in the cells.

PRINTING

Alright. That was the basics of manipulating your data. Now on to printing. You might not think that printing needs its own chapter, but it does. Not because clicking on Print is so hard to do, but because you need to format your data well to get it to print well. If you just hit print without thinking about how that information in your worksheet will appear on a page, you'll likely end up with pages worth of poorly-formatted garbage.

Now, it's possible you have no intent of printing anything, in which case, skip this chapter. But if you are going to print, let's try and waste as little paper as possible for you.

First things first. To print, go to the File tab and select Print. If you don't want to clean anything up, you can then just click on the big Print button right there on the page and be done with it.

Typing Ctrl and P at the same time (Ctrl + P) will also take you to the print screen which looks like this:

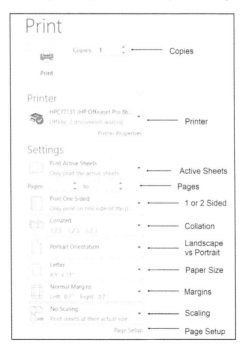

There are a number of things you can do on this page, so let's just walk through them starting at the top and working our way down.

Print

Once you're ready to print your page, you can click on the button on the top left with the image of a printer that says Print.

Number of Copies

If you want to print more than one copy, change your number of copies using the up and down arrows next to the Print button.

Printer

It should display your computer's default printer, but if you want to use a different printer than that one, click on the arrow next to the printer name and choose from the listed options. If the printer you want isn't listed, choose Add Printer and add the printer.

Print Active Sheets / Print Entire Workbook / Print Selection

My version of Excel defaults to Print Active Sheets. This will generally be the worksheet you were working in when you chose to print. However, you can select more than one worksheet by holding down the Control key and then clicking on another worksheet's name. When you do this, you'll see that the names of all of your selected worksheets are highlighted, not just one of them.

I would only print multiple worksheets if you're satisfied that each one is formatted the way you want it formatted. Also, choosing to print more than one sheet at a time either with Print Active Sheets or Print Entire Workbook, results in strange things happening to your headers and footers. For example, your page numbering will occur across worksheets. If you mean each worksheet to be a standalone report with numbered pages specific to that report, then you need to print each worksheet separately.

As I just alluded to, the Print Entire Workbook option prints all of the worksheets in your workbook.

Print Selection allows you to just print a highlighted section of a worksheet or worksheets. (I happened to have three worksheets selected at once and when I highlighted the first twenty cells in one of those worksheets, the selection it was ready to print was those twenty cells in each of the three worksheets.)

Print Selected Pages

Just below the Print Active Sheets section is a row that says Pages and has two boxes with arrows at the side. You can choose to just print a specific page rather than the entire worksheet. To figure out which page to print, look at your preview (which should be taking up most of the screen).

Print One Sided / Print on Both Sides (long edge) / Print on Both Sides (short edge)

The default is to just print on one side of your paper. If you have a printer that can print on both sides of the page you can change your settings to do so. You want the long-edge option if your layout is going to be portrait-style and the short-edge option if your layout is going to be landscape-style. (See below.)

Collated / Uncollated

This only matters if what you're printing has more than one page and if you're printing more than one copy. In that case, you need to decide if you want to print one full copy at a time, x number of times or if you want to print x copies of page 1 and then x copies of page 2 and then x copies of page 3 and so on until you've printed all pages of your document. In general, I would choose collated, which is also the default.

Portrait Orientation / Landscape Orientation

You can choose to print in either portrait orientation (with the short edge of the page on top) or landscape orientation (with the long edge of the page on top). You can see the difference by changing the option in Excel and looking at your print preview.

Which option you choose will depend mostly on how many columns of data you have.

Assuming I'm dealing with a normal worksheet with rows of data listed across various columns, my goal is to fit all of my columns on one page if possible. Sometimes changing the layout to landscape allows me to do that because it allows me to have more columns per page than I'd be able to fit in portrait mode.

If I have just a few columns of data, but lots of rows I'll generally stick with portrait orientation instead.

You'll have to decide what works best for you and your specific data.

Letter / Legal / Statement / Etc.

This is where you select your paper type. Unless you're in an office or overseas, chances are you'll leave this exactly like it is. I'm sure my printer could print on legal paper, but I don't have any for it to use so it's a moot point for me. In an office you may have the choice of 8.5"x11", legal paper, and even other larger sizes than that.

Normal Margins / Wide Margins / Narrow Margins / Custom Margins

I would expect you won't use this, but if you need to then this would be where you can change the margins on the document. The normal margins allow for .7" on each side and .75" on top and bottom. If you have a lot of text and need just a little more room to fit it all on one page, you could use the narrow margin option to make that happen. I generally use the scaling option instead.

No Scaling / Fit Sheet on One Page /
Fit All Columns on One Page / Fit All Rows on One Page

I use this option often when I have a situation where my columns are just a little bit too much to fit on the page or my rows go just a little bit beyond the page. If you choose "Fit All Columns on One Page" that will make sure that all of your columns fit across the top of one page. You might still have multiple pages because of the number of rows, but at least everything will fit across one page.

Of course, depending on how many columns you have, this might not be a good choice. Excel will make it fit, but it will do so by decreasing your font size and if you have too many columns you're trying to fit on one page your font size may become so small you can't read it.

So be sure to look at your preview before you print. (And use Landscape Orientation first if you need to.)

Fit All Rows on One Page is good for if you have maybe one or two rows too many to naturally fit on the page.

Fit Sheet on One Page is a combination of fitting all columns and all rows onto one page. Again, Excel will do it if you ask it to, but with a large set of data you won't be able to read it.

Page Setup

The Page Setup link at the very bottom gives you access to even more options. As with everything else in the more modern versions of Excel, the most obvious options are the ones that are readily visible that we already discussed, but there are other options you have in formatting your page. If you click on the Page Setup link you'll be taken to the Page Setup dialogue box which is another way to choose all your print options. A few things to point out to you that I find useful:

1. **Scaling**

On the Page tab you can see the scaling option once more. But the nice thing here is that you can fit your information to however many pages across by however many pages long. You're not limited to 1 page wide or 1 page tall. So say you have a document that's currently one page wide and four pages long but the last page is just one row. You can scale that document in the Page Setup dialogue box so that the document that prints is one page wide by three pages long and that last row is brought up onto the prior page.

2. **Center Horizontally or Vertically**

On the Margins tabs there are two check boxes that let you center what you're printing either horizontally or vertically or both. I will often choose to center an item vertically. If I don't do that, it tends to looks off balance.

3. **Header/Footer**

We're going to talk about another way to do this in a moment, but if you want to setup a header and/or a footer for your printed document you can do so here. The dropdown boxes that say (none) include a number of pre-formatted headers and footers for you to use. So if you just want the page number included, there should be a pre-formatted one that lets you do that. Same with including the worksheet name or file name in the header or footer. As you look at each one it will show you examples of the actual text that will be included. You also have the option of customizing either the header or footer.

4. Sheet

The sheet tab has a couple of useful options, but I'm going to show you a different way to set these options because I find it easier to set them when I'm in the worksheet itself.

* * *

Page Layout Tab

If you exit out of the print option and go back to your worksheet, you'll see that one of the tabs you have available to use is called Page Layout. There are certain attributes that I set up here before I print my documents. Let's walk through them.

(Also, note that you can change margins, orientation, and size here just as easily as in the print preview screen.)

1. Print Area

If you only want to print a portion of a worksheet, you can set that portion as your print area by highlighting it, and then clicking on the arrow next to Print Area and choosing Set Print Area.

Only do it this way (as opposed to highlighting the section and choosing Print-Selection) if it's a permanent setting. Once you set your print area it will remain set until you clear it. You can add more data to your worksheet but it will never print until you change your print area or clear the setting.

I use this when I have a worksheet that has either a lot of extra information I don't want to print or where the formatting extends beyond my data and Excel keeps trying to print all those empty but formatted cells.

2. Breaks

You can set where a page break occurs in your worksheet. So say you have a worksheet that takes up four pages and you want to make sure that rows 1 through 10 are on a page together and then rows 11 through 20 are on a page together even though that's not how things would naturally fall. You can set a page break to force that to happen.

Personally, I find page breaks a challenge to work with, so I usually try to get what I need some other way.

3. Print Titles

This one is incredibly valuable. When you click on it, you'll see that it brings up the Page Setup box and takes you to the Sheet tab.

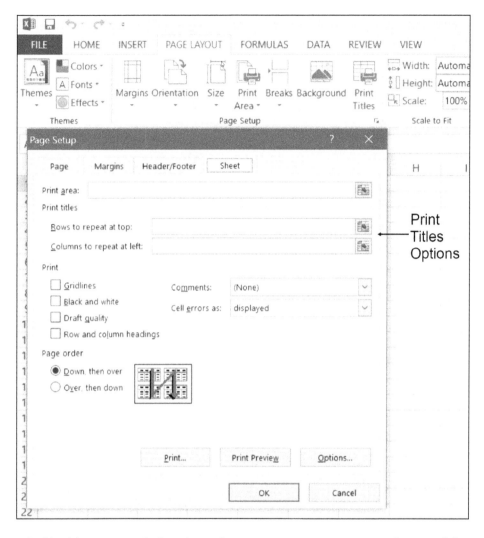

The first valuable thing you can do here is set the rows you want to repeat at the top of the page. Say you have a worksheet with a thousand rows of data in it that will print on a hundred pages. How do you know what's in each column on each page? You need a header row. And you need that header row to repeat at the top of each and every page.

"Rows to repeat at top" is where you specify what row(s) is your header row. Click in that box and then click on the row number in your worksheet that you want to have repeat at the top of each page.

The second valuable thing you can do here is set a column(s) you want to repeat on the left-hand side of each page. I need this one less often, but I do still sometimes use it. Say, for example, that you had a list of students, one per row, and their test scores across fifty tests, and that when you printed that information it printed across two pages. Well, without listing the student's name in the left-hand column on every page, you wouldn't know whose scores you were looking at after the first page. So you'd need to set that name column to repeat on each page.

To do so, click in the box that says "Columns to repeat at left", and then click on the letter for the column(s) you want to repeat on each page.

You'll see that Excel converts your choices to standard notation, so if you feel comfortable enough you can just type it in yourself, but I almost never do.

Do be careful if you're going to choose more than one row or column to repeat that you don't end up selecting so many rows or columns that you basically just print the same thing over and over and over again.

CONCLUSION

There you have it. A beginner's guide to Excel. This wasn't meant to be a comprehensive guide to Excel, but to instead give you the basics you need to do 95% of what you'll ever want to do in Excel. I hope it did that.

If something wasn't clear or you have any questions, please feel free to reach out to me at mlhumphreywriter@gmail.com. I don't check that email daily, but I do check it regularly and am happy to help.

Also, if there was something I didn't cover that you want to know about, the Microsoft website has a number of tutorials and examples that I think are very well-written and easy to follow at www.suppport.office.com. I usually find what I need with a quick internet search for something like "bold text Excel 2013" and then choose the Microsoft link

I find their web-based help much more useful than the Help options available within Excel, but you can try those, too. Click on the question mark in the top right corner and search for what you need. Or you can hold your mouse over the tasks listed on the various tabs and you'll usually see a brief description of what the item does. A lot of the descriptions also have a "tell me more" link at the bottom of the description that will take you directly to the help screen related to that item.

If you want to explore more advanced uses of Excel and liked the way I present information, then check out *Intermediate Excel* which explores topics such as pivot tables, charts, conditional formatting, IF functions, and a lot more. (The full list is included in the introduction to the book.)

I've also published a few hands-on guides that might interest you.

The *Juggling Your Finances: Basic Excel Primer* focuses on how to use addition, subtraction, division, and multiplication to manage your personal finances and walks you through a number of sample calculations. The focus there is just on those four functions and how to use them.

Excel for Writers and *Excel for Self-Publishers* are geared towards writers and assume that you're comfortable with Excel. They walk users through exactly how to create things like a word count and time tracker or a two-variable analysis grid right down to how to format the cells to match the examples and what each formula needs to be in each cell. Sometimes the challenge with Excel is in figuring out how to use it to do what you want and that's what those guides cover.

Again, if there's something specific you want to know how to do, just ask. Happy to point you in the right direction.

And thanks for reading this guide. Excel is an incredibly powerful tool and now that you have the foundation you need to use it effectively, I hope you'll see just how incredible it can be.

Also, if you want to test your knowledge of this material check out *The Excel for Beginners Quiz Book* which contains quizzes for each section of this book as well as five exercises that will allow you to apply what you've learned here in real-world scenarios.

INDEX

INDEX (CONTINUED)

CONTROL SHORTCUTS

For each of the control shortcuts, hold down Ctrl and the key listed to perform the command.

Command	Ctrl +
Select All	A
Bold	B
Copy	C
Find	F
Replace	H
Italicize	I
Print	P
Next Worksheet	Page Down
Prior Worksheet	Page Up
Save	S
Underline	U
Paste	V
Cut	X
Redo	Y
Undo	Z

Word for Beginners

WORD ESSENTIALS BOOK 1

M.L. HUMPHREY

CONTENTS

INTRODUCTION

The purpose of this guide is to introduce you to the basics of using Microsoft Word. While there are a number of other word processing programs out there, Word is still the gold-standard go-to program in use in large portions of the corporate world, so if you're going to be involved in a white collar job (and even some blue collar jobs), being familiar with Word will be a significant advantage for you. And essential for many jobs. (The days of having an assistant who could do those things for you are gone.)

It's also the program I use for all of my writing. (This book isn't going to be focused on self-publishing, but if you format a document the right way in Word you can publish directly to most of the major sales platforms without any additional effort.)

Word can be incredibly simple to use. At its most basic, you can open a new file, type in your text, save, and be done. But chances are that you'll want more control over what you type and how it looks than that. Maybe you need to use a different font or font size. Maybe you want to indent your paragraphs. Maybe you want to include a bulleted or numbered list in your document.

That's where this guide comes in. I'll walk you through the absolute basics (open, save, delete), too, but most of this guide will be focused on what to do with your text once it's been typed into your document.

Having said that, we're not going to cover everything you can do in Word. The goal of this guide is to get you up to speed and comfortable with what you'll need for probably 98% of what you'll use Word for on a daily basis.

The exceptions to that are if you're working in an environment where you need to use track changes to work on a group document or one where you need to create tables or complex multilevel lists. Those are more advanced topics that are covered in *Intermediate Word*.

The goal here is to give you a solid foundation that you can work from, and I don't want to distract from those core skills by getting into specialized topics that either won't apply to most users or that require enough detail to understand that they'll likely confuse a beginning user.

Another thing to note before we get started. All of the screenshots I'm going to show you are from Word 2013. If you have an earlier version of Word, especially a version prior to 2007, things may look different at the top of the screen. All of the shortcut keys, which I would recommend you use, will be the same, but navigation won't be.

With Excel I recommend that people with older versions upgrade to a post-2007 version of the program. With Word, especially for the beginner level, that probably isn't necessary. However, if you're using a really old version of Word you're going to have less help options. Right now the Microsoft website only has tutorials for Word 2010, 2013, and 2016, and most users won't have access to your version of Word to be able to see what you're seeing.

If you're using Word 2016, nothing we're going to cover here appears to have changed with the most recent version, so you should be fine.

Alright then. Ready? Let's do this.

BASIC TERMINOLOGY

Before we get started, I want to make sure that we're on the same page in terms of terminology.

TAB

I refer to the menu choices at the top of the screen (File, Home, Insert, Design, Page Layout, References, Mailings, Review, View, Developer) as tabs. If you click on one you'll see that the way it's highlighted sort of looks like an old-time filing system.

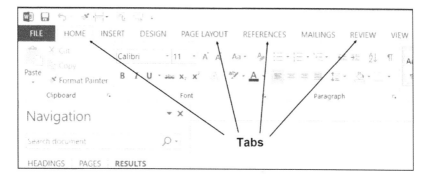

Each tab you select will show you different options. For example, in the image above, I have the Home tab selected and you can do various tasks such as cut/copy/paste, format paint, change the font, change the formatting of a paragraph, apply a style to your text, find/replace words in your document, or select the text in your document. Other tabs give other options.

CLICK

If I tell you to click on something, that means to use your mouse (or trackpad) to move the arrow on the screen over to a specific location and left-click or right-click on the option. (See the next definition for the difference between left-click and right-click).

If you left-click, this selects the item. If you right-click, this generally creates a dropdown list of options to choose from. If I don't tell you which to do, left- or right-click, then left-click.

LEFT-CLICK/RIGHT-CLICK

If you look at your mouse or your trackpad, you generally have two flat buttons to press. One is on the left side, one is on the right. If I say left-click that means to press down on the button on the left. If I say right-click that means press down on the button on the right.

Now, as I sadly learned when I had to upgrade computers and ended up with an HP Envy, not all track pads have the left- and right-hand buttons. In that case, you'll basically want to press on either the bottom left-hand side of the track pad or the bottom right-hand side of the trackpad. Since you're working blind it may take a little trial and error to get the option you want working. (Or is that just me?)

SELECT OR HIGHLIGHT

If I tell you to select text, that means to left-click at the end of the text you want to select, hold that left-click, and move your cursor to the other end of the text you want to select.

Another option is to use the Shift key. Go to one end of the text you want to select. Hold down the shift key and use the arrow keys to move to the other end of the text you want to select. If you arrow up or down, that will select an entire row at a time.

With both methods, which side of the text you start on doesn't matter. You can start at the end and go to the beginning or start at the beginning and go to the end. Just start at one end or the other of the text you want to select.

The text you've selected will then be highlighted in gray. Like the words "sample text" in this image:

This is **sample text** so you can see what I'm talking about.

If you need to select text that isn't touching you can do this by selecting your first section of text and then holding down the Ctrl key and selecting your second section of text using your mouse. (You can't arrow to the second section of text or you'll lose your already selected text.)

DROPDOWN MENU

If you right-click in a Word document, you will see what I'm going to refer to as a dropdown menu. (Sometimes it will actually drop upward if you're towards the bottom of the document.)

A dropdown menu provides you a list of choices to select from.

There are also dropdown menus available for some of the options listed under the tabs at the top of the screen. For example, if you go to the Home tab, you'll see small arrows below or next to some of the options, like the numbered list option in the paragraph section. If you click on those arrows, you'll see that there are multiple choices you can choose from listed on a dropdown menu.

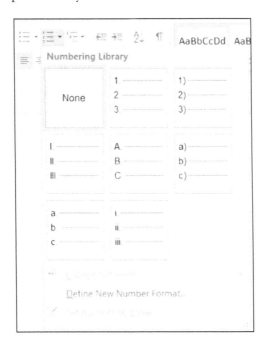

EXPANSION ARROWS

I don't know the official word for these, but you'll also notice at the bottom right corner of most of the sections in each tab that there are little arrows. If you hold your mouse over the arrow it lets you bring up a more detailed set of options, usually through a dialogue box (which we'll discuss next).

In the Home tab, for example, there are expansion arrows for Clipboard, Font, Paragraph, and Styles. Holding your mouse over the arrow will give a brief description of what clicking on the expansion arrow will do.

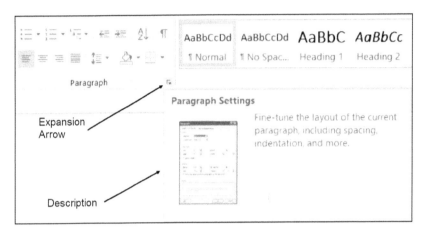

DIALOGUE BOX

Dialogue boxes are pop-up boxes that cover specialized settings. As just mentioned, if you click on an expansion arrow, it will often open a dialogue box that contains more choices than are visible in that section. When you right-click in a Word document and choose Font, Paragraph, or Hyperlink that also opens dialogue boxes. Dialogue boxes allow the most granular level of control over an option

This is the Replace dialogue box.

This may not apply to you, but be aware that if you have more than one Word document open and open a dialogue box in one of those documents, you may not be able to move to the other documents you have open until you close the dialogue box.

SCROLL BAR

This is more useful in Excel than in Word, but on the right-hand side of the screen you should see a scroll bar. You can either click in the space above or below the bar to move up or down a small amount or you can left-click on the bar, hold the left-click, and drag the bar up or down to move through the document more quickly. You can also use the arrows at the top and the bottom to move up and down through your document. (The scroll bar isn't always visible in Word. If you don't see it, move your mouse over to the side of the screen and it should appear.)

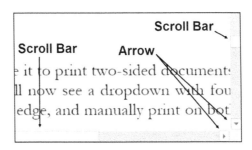

In general, you shouldn't see a scroll bar at the bottom of the screen, but it is possible. This would happen if you ever change the zoom level of your document to the point that you're not seeing the entire width of the document in a single screen. (Not something I recommend when working with normal documents.)

ARROW

If I ever tell you to arrow to the left or right or up or down, that just means use your arrow keys. This will move your cursor to the left one space, to the right one space, up one line, or down one line. If you're at the end of a line and arrow to the right, it will take you to the beginning of the next line. If you're at the beginning of a line and arrow to the left, it will take you to the end of the last line.

CURSOR

There are two possible meanings for cursor. One is the one I just used. In your Word document, you will see that there is a blinking line. This indicates where you are in the document. If you type text, each letter will appear where the cursor was at the time you typed it. The cursor will move (at least in the U.S. and I'd assume most European versions) to the right as you type. This version of the cursor should be visible at all times unless you have text selected.

The other type of cursor is the one that's tied to the movement of your mouse or trackpad. When you're typing, it will not be visible. But stop typing and move your mouse or trackpad, and you'll see it. If the cursor is positioned over your text, it will look somewhat like a tall skinny capital I. If you move it up to the menu options or off to the sides, it becomes a white arrow. (Except for when you position it over any option under the tabs that can be typed in such as Font Size or Font where it will once again look like a skinny capital I.)

Usually I won't refer to your cursor, I'll just say, "click" or "select" or whatever action you need to take with it, but moving the cursor to that location will be implied.

QUICK ACCESS TOOLBAR

You might notice that the options in the very top left corner of my version of Word are different from what you see. That's because I've customized the Quick Access Toolbar. You can do this on your version of Word by clicking on the arrow you see at the very end of the list and then checking the commands you want to have available there. It can be useful if there's something you're doing repeatedly (like inserting section breaks) that's located on a different tab than something else you're doing repeatedly (like formatting text).

Of course, it's only useful if you use it. Half the time I forget I've done that. But if you can remember, it's a nice time-saver.

CONTROL SHORTCUTS

Throughout this document, I'm going to mention various control shortcuts that you can use to perform tasks like save, copy, cut, and paste. (There's a list of the most important ones in the appendix.) Each of these will be written as Ctrl + a capital letter, but when you use the shortcut on your computer you don't need to use the capitalized version of the letter. For example, holding down the Ctrl key and the s key at the same time will save your document. I'll write this as Ctrl + S, but that just means hold down the key that says ctrl and the s key at the same time.

ABSOLUTE BASICS

Before we do anything else, there are a few absolute basics that we should cover.

STARTING A NEW WORD FILE

To start a brand new Word file, I click on Word 2013 from my applications menu or the shortcut I have on my computer's taskbar. If you're already in Word and want to open a new Word file, go to the File tab and choose New from the left-hand menu.

Whichever option you choose will bring up a list of various templates, including the first option which is for a "Blank document". Ninety-nine percent of the time that's the one you'll want. To use it, left-click on the image.

OPENING AN EXISTING WORD FILE

To open an existing Word file you can either go to the folder where the file is saved and double-click on the file name, or (if Word is already open) go to the File tab and choose Open from the left-hand menu. Or you can just open Word without selecting a file and it will provide a list of recent documents to choose from on the left-hand side.

If you're in Word and the document you need is listed, left-click on it once and it will open as long as you haven't renamed the file or moved it since it was last open. (In that case, you'll need to navigate to where the file is saved and open it that way, either through Word or outside of Word.)

To navigate to the file you need, click on Open Other Documents and then click on Computer under Open (if you just opened Word and don't have any files open) or click on Computer under Home (if you already had a file open).

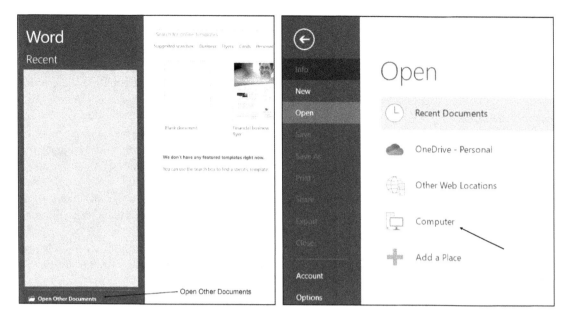

This should give you a list of recent folders you've used or you can click on Browse if the file you need isn't in one of those folders. When you click on Browse this will bring up the Open dialogue box (below). From there you can navigate to any location on your computer.

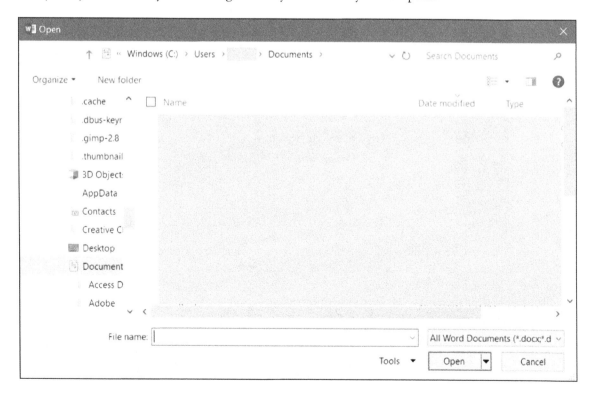

SAVING A WORD FILE

To quickly save a document, you can use Ctrl + S or click on the small image of a floppy disk in the top left corner of the screen above File. For a document you've already saved that will overwrite the prior version of the document with the current version and will keep the file name, file type, and file location the same.

If you try to save a file that has never been saved before, it will automatically default to the Save As option which requires that you specify where to save the file, give it a name, and designate the file type. There are defaults for name and format, but you'll want to change the name of the document to something better than Document2.

You can also choose Save As when you want to change the location of a file, the name of a file, or the file type. (With respect to file type, I sometimes need to, for example, save a .doc file as a .pdf file or a .doc file as a .docx file for use with certain formatting programs.)

The first choice you have to make for Save As is where you want to save the file. I see a list of my most recent six folders listed and can also choose to Browse if I want to use a different location than one of the folders listed.

When you click on the location where you want to save the file, this will bring up the Save As dialogue box. Type in the name you want for the file and choose the file type. My file type defaults to Word 97-2003 Document (.doc) which is the format I prefer to save in because it's the easiest format for all users and all versions of Word to open. If you save as a .docx file you may encounter situations where someone you share the file with won't be able to open it.

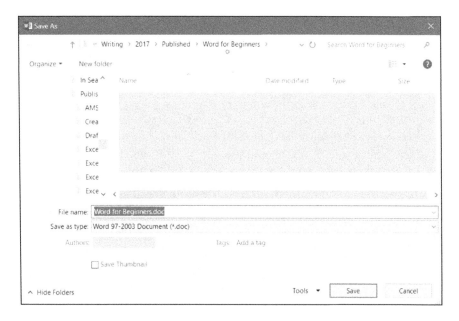

If you had already saved the file and you choose to Save As but keep the same location, name, and format as before, Word will overwrite the previous version of the file just like it would have if you'd used Save.

If you just want to rename a file, it's actually best to close the file and then go to where the file is saved and rename it that way rather than use Save As. Using Save As will keep the original of the file as well as creating the newer version. That's great when you want version control (which I often need), but not when you just wanted to rename your file from Great Book Version 22 to Great Book FINAL.

RENAMING A WORD FILE

As discussed above, you can use Save As to give an existing file a new name, but that approach will leave you with two versions of the file, one with the old name and one with the new name. If you just want to change the name of the existing file, close it and then navigate to where you've saved it. Click on the file name once to select it, click on it a second time to highlight the name, and then type in the new name you want to use, replacing the old one. If you rename the file this way outside of Word, there will only be one version of the file left, the one with the new name you wanted.

Just be aware that if you rename a file by navigating to where it's located and changing the name you won't be able to access the file from the Recent Workbooks listing under Open file, since that will still list the old name which no longer exists.

DELETING A WORD FILE

You can't delete a Word file from within Word. You need to close the file you want to delete and then navigate to where the file is stored and delete the file there without opening it. Once you've located the file, click on the file name. (Only enough to select it. Make sure you haven't double-clicked and highlighted the name which will delete the file name but not the file.) Next, choose

Delete from the menu at the top of the screen, or right-click and choose Delete from the dropdown menu.

CLOSING A WORD FILE

To close a Word file click on the X in the top right corner or go to File and then choose Close. (You can also use Ctrl + W, but I never have.)

If no changes have been made to the document since you saved it last, it will just close.

If changes have been made, Word should ask you if you want to save those changes. You can either choose to save them, not save them, or cancel closing the document and leave it open. I almost always default to saving any changes. If I'm in doubt about whether I'd be overwriting something important, I cancel and choose to Save As and save the current file as a later version of the document just in case (e.g., Great Book v2).

If you had copied an image or a large block of text, you may also have a box pop up asking if you want to keep that image or text when you close the document. Usually the answer to this is no, but if you had planned on pasting that image or text somewhere else and hadn't yet done so, you can say to keep it on the clipboard.

BASIC TASKS

At its most basic, adding text into a Word document is incredibly simple. You simply open a new document and start typing. When you're done, you save the document.

Go ahead and do it. See? Open. Type. Save. Voila.

But you probably want to do more with your text than that. And we'll cover all the formatting, which is the majority of what you'll want to do, in the next section. First, I want to cover a few basic functions that you can perform in Word that will make your life easier as you enter your text and then edit it.

UNDO

Undo lets you take the last thing (or few things) you did, and undo it. That means you don't have to be afraid to try something that you're not sure will work, because you can always reverse it.

To undo something, simply type Ctrl + Z. If you did a few things you didn't like, just keep typing Ctrl + Z until they're all gone. But beware that Word undoes things in order, so if you want to undo the second-to-last thing you did, you'll have to first undo the last thing you did.

REDO

If you take it too far and undo too much and want something back, then you can choose to redo. That's done by typing Ctrl + Y. Go ahead and try it out. Type a sentence in your document. Undo it with Ctrl + Z and then redo it with Ctrl + Y. Easy peasy.

(If you don't want to use control keys, you can also add undo and redo to the Quick Access Toolbar, but I'd highly recommend that you memorize these two. You'll work much faster if you can memorize the control key shortcuts for undo, redo, save, copy, cut, and paste.)

DELETE

Another basic task you need to master is how to delete text. There are a few ways to do this. If you're trying to delete something that you just typed, use the backspace key to delete the letters one at a time.

You can also place the cursor next to the text you want to delete and then use the backspace or delete keys, depending on where the cursor is relative to the text you're trying to delete. If your cursor is on the left-hand side of text, use the delete key. On the right-hand side, use the backspace key. (And if you get it wrong, remember that you have Ctrl + Z to undo what you just did.)

If you want to delete a large chunk of text at one time, select the text you want to delete and then use the delete OR backspace key.

SELECT ALL

The other basic task that you should know about before we start talking formatting is how to select all of the text in your document.

Select All is very useful for applying a format to your entire document. I tend to write in the default font that Word uses and then change the font once I'm done. It's also handy if you want to copy the contents of one document into another. Say, for example, you worked on a group project and each person wrote their individual piece in a separate document and now you need to combine them. Or, like me, you wrote your first novel using separate files for each chapter (Don't do that, by the way.) You can take those final documents, select all, copy, and paste into one master document that combines them.

To Select All, go to the Home tab and then to the Editing section on the far right-hand side and click on the arrow next to Select. In the dropdown menu choose Select All.

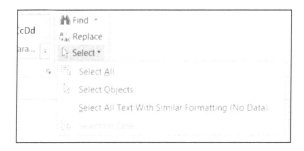

Another option is to use Ctrl + A, although I don't consider this one of the control shortcuts that I use often enough to memorize.

I've also added Select All as one of my Quick Access Toolbar options.

If you ever choose all of the text in a document and then decide you didn't want to, just click somewhere in the document and the selection will go away. (You can also arrow up or down, but that will take you to the top or the bottom of the document and you may not want that.)

COPYING, CUTTING, AND PASTING

Copy and Cut are similar. They're both a way to move text from one location to another. Copy leaves the text where it was and creates a copy of that text to move to the new location. Cut removes the text from where it was and puts the text on a "clipboard" (that's usually not visible to you) for movement to a new location.

Paste is how you tell Word where that new location is.

The first step in copying or cutting text is to select all of the text you want to move. To select text you can left-click on one side of the text, hold down that left-click and move your mouse or trackpad until all of the text you want is highlighted. Or you can use the shift key and the arrow keys to select your text.

Once your text is selected, to copy it type Ctrl + C or to cut it type Ctrl + X.

If you don't want to use the control shortcuts, you can also go to the Home tab and in the Clipboard section choose Copy or Cut from there. Or you can right-click after you've selected your text and choose Copy or Cut from the dropdown menu.

I recommend using the control shortcuts, because it's the fastest and these three commands are ones you'll use often enough to make it worth memorizing them.

If you copy text, it remains visible in the location you copied it from. Behind the scenes Word has taken a copy of that text and placed it on a "clipboard" for use elsewhere.

If you cut text, the text is immediately removed from the document. It too is placed on a "clipboard" for use elsewhere. (This also means that cut text, if you choose not to paste it somewhere else, is deleted text.)

To see the clipboard where the items you've copied or cut are stored, go to the Home tab and click on the expansion arrow next to Clipboard. This will bring up a Clipboard display with all of the items you've recently copied or cut from your document.

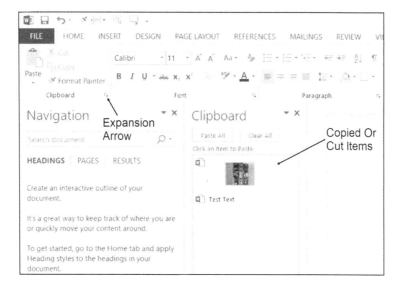

As you can see here, I copied two snippets of text as well as took a screenshot. I could use this clipboard to paste all of those items into my document at once using that Paste All option. (This wasn't always an available option in Word so if you have a really old version you won't be able to see or do this.)

You can also just click on one of the items and it will paste into your document. This can come in handy if you have something you need to paste more than once into your document, but usually you won't need this. You'll just want to copy or cut one item and then paste it into another spot in your document (or another document) right then.

The simplest way to paste something you've just copied or cut is to use Ctrl + V. Simply copy or cut your item, go to where you want to place it, type Ctrl + V, and you're done.

Your other two options are to go to the Clipboard section of the Home tab and click on Paste. Or you can right-click and choose one of the Paste options from the dropdown menu in the document.

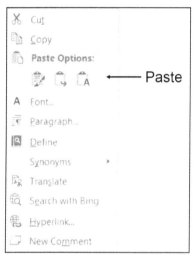

PASTE OPTIONS

If you use Ctrl + V to paste text, you'll be pasting not only the text you copied or cut, but its formatting as well. Usually, that's fine and you'll probably be able to use Ctrl + V ninety-five percent of the time. (And even if you don't want to keep the formatting, there's a trick I'll show you later—using the Format Painter—that you can use to quickly correct formatting after you paste the text into its new location. All it requires is that you have some text that's already formatted the way you want.)

But sometimes you'll want to paste the text in without that formatting. That's where using the Paste dropdown menus comes in handy, because they allow you to choose how you paste your item.

As you can see in the images above, once you've copied or cut an item, you'll be given three paste options: Keep Source Formatting, Merge Formatting, and Keep Text Only. (They're represented by small images, but if you hold your mouse over each one, you'll be able to see the labels.)

In the image below I've pasted the red and bolded word TEST written in Calibri font into a sentence written in black font in Times New Roman using each paste option. This shows how text in a different color, font, and bolding is handled under each paste option.

TEST

Ctrl + V (Paste)

Sample **TEST** text for demonstration purposes.

Keep Source Formatting

Sample **TEST** text for demonstration purposes.

Merge Formatting

Sample **TEST** text for demonstration purposes.

Keep Text Only

Sample TEST text for demonstration purposes.

Using Ctrl + V, the color, font, and bolding of the original text remain.

Using Keep Source Formatting gives the same result. Color, font, and bolding are the same as the original text.

With Merge Formatting the color and font of the original text are lost, but the bolding of the original text is not. So "TEST" is now in Times New Roman and black, but it's still bolded.

Using Keep Text Only the color, font, and bolding of the original text are all lost and replaced with the color, font, and bolding (in this case none) of the destination text.

That may seem a little confusing, and honestly, my recommendation is to just use Ctrl + V and fix the formatting after the text is in your document. The main time I use these other paste options is when copying from websites that use hyperlinks that I don't want to bring into my document. Then I paste using Keep Text Only.

If you remember anything from what we just walked through, remember this:

Ctrl + C to copy.

Ctrl + X to cut.

Ctrl + V to paste.

TEXT FORMATTING

Now that you know how to create a file, enter the text you want, and save your work, it's time to actually format that text. Let's start with font.

CHOOSING A FONT – GENERAL THOUGHTS

The font you use governs the general appearance of the text in your document. My version of Word uses Calibri font as the default, but there are hundreds of fonts you can choose. Here is a sample of a few of those choices:

Sans-Serif Examples:
Calibri
Arial
Gill Sans MT
Serif Font Examples:
Times New Roman
Garamond
Palatino Linotype

The first three samples are sans-serif fonts. (That just means they don't have little feet at the bottom of the letters.) The second three samples are serif fonts. (They do have those little feet at the bottom of each letter.) All of these fonts are the same size, but you can see that the different fonts have a different appearance and take up different amounts of space on the page. Arial is darker and taller than Calibri, for example.

Many companies and teachers will specify the font you need to use. If they don't I'd suggest using a serifed font like Garamond or Times New Roman for text since serifed fonts are supposed to be easier to read.

And unless you're working on a creative project, don't get too fancy with your fonts. The six listed in that example above should cover almost any text needs you have. At the end of the day, the goal is for someone to be able to read what you've written. So no Algerian in many body text. Save those fonts for embellishments and section labels.

CHANGING THE FONT

There are a few ways you can change the font in your document. If you already know you want to use a different font, it's easiest to do so before you start typing. Otherwise you'll need to select all of the text you want to change. (Either with Select All if it's all text in the document or by selecting chunks of text and changing them one chunk at a time.)

The first way to change the font is to go to the Font section of the Home tab. Click on the arrow to the right of the current font name and choose from the dropdown menu.

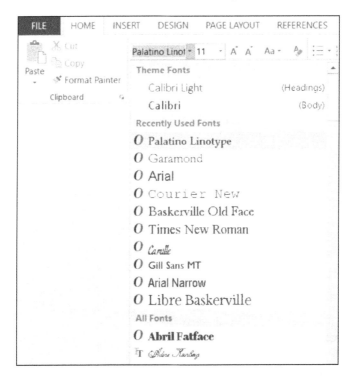

The first section of the dropdown menu lists the fonts for the theme you're using. Usually that'll be the defaults for Word, in this case, Calibri and Calibri Light. Next you'll see Recently Used Fonts. Most of the time there will only be one or two fonts here, but I had used a number recently.

Finally, you'll see a list of all available fonts in alphabetical order. If you know the font you want, you can start typing in its name rather than scroll through the entire list. Otherwise, use the scroll bar on the right-hand side to move through the list. Each font is written using the font to give you an idea what it will look like. See in the example the difference between Algerian and Garamond?

The next way to change your font is to right-click and choose Font from the dropdown menu. This will bring up the Font dialogue box. In the top left corner you can choose the font you want.

There's a third option for changing the font, something I'm going to call the mini formatting menu, in the newest versions of Word. To see this menu, right-click in your document or select a section of text using your mouse. When you select a section of text, a smaller version of the Font section of the Home tab will appear just above your text. If you right-click it will appear above the dropdown menu.

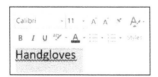

As you can see, one of the options that you can change in the mini formatting menu is the font. (If the font name box is empty, that's because you have text selected and there's more than one font in the selection.) To change the font, click on the arrow to the right of the listed font and choose the one you want from the dropdown just like you would in the Font section of the Home tab. I would recommend that you only use this option for a selection of text that you want to change to a new font. It's much better to change the font for your document in the Home tab.

FONT SIZE

Font size dictates how large the text will be. Here are some examples of different font sizes:

8 pt   12 pt   16 pt

As you can see, the larger the font size, the larger the text. Most documents are written in a ten, eleven, or twelve point font size. Often footnotes or endnotes will use eight or nine point. Chapter headings or title pages will use the larger font sizes. Whatever font size you do use, try to be consistent between different sections of your document. So all main body text should use just one font size. Same for chapter or section headings.

Changing the font size works much the same way as changing the font. You have the same three options: You can go to the Font section of the Home tab, bring up the mini formatting menu by right-clicking, or bring up the Font dialogue box by right-clicking and choosing Font from the dropdown menu. If you want to change existing text, you need to select the text first. If you want to change the font size for text that you're going to type, do so with the Home tab or the Font dialogue box options.

For all three options the font size is listed to the right of the font name.

For the Home tab or mini formatting menu options, you can click on the arrow next to the current font size to bring up a dropdown menu that lets you choose your font size. In the Font dialogue box that list of choices is already visible.

If the font size you want isn't listed, you can type it in instead. Just click into the box for font size and change the number to the font size you want to use.

In the Home tab and the mini formatting menu, if you're only changing the font by one or two point sizes, you can instead use the increase and decrease font options directly to the right of the font size. These are depicted as the letter A with a small arrow above it. The one on the left is an arrow that points upward (to increase the font size). The one on the right is an arrow that points downward (to decrease the font size). If you use the increase/decrease font options, they increase and decrease the font size one place according to the font sizes listed in the dropdown menu.

Here is an image of all three choices for changing font size in the Home tab.

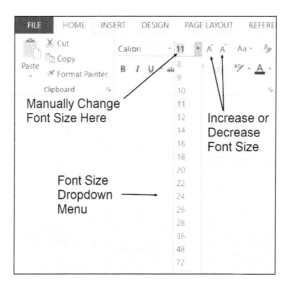

FONT COLOR

Changing your font color works the same as changing your font or font size. Select the text you want to change and then either go to the Font section of the Home tab, pull up the mini formatting menu, or right-click and choose Font from the dropdown menu to bring up the Font dialogue box. This time, though, you want to click on the arrow next to the A with the solid colored line under it in the bottom right corner of the section:

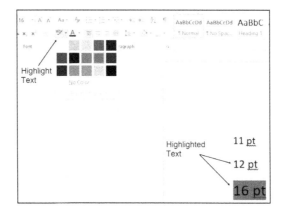

This will give you a dropdown menu with seventy different colors to choose from. Click on the color you want and it will change your text to that color.

If those seventy choices are not enough, you can click on More Colors at the bottom of the dropdown box. This will bring up the Colors dialogue box where you can choose from even more colors or specify a specific color in the Custom tab using RGB values. (Not likely to be needed for a font color, but this does come into play for fill color and is discussed in more detail in *Intermediate Word*.)

HIGHLIGHTING TEXT

Another thing you can do is highlight text in a document much like you might do with a highlighter. You can do this from the Font section of the Home tab or in the mini formatting menu. Select the text you want to highlight and then look for the letters ab and what looks like a pen running diagonally right to left between the ab and a colored line:

If you want to highlight using the color shown in the line, you can just click on the image. If you want to use a different color, left-click on the arrow and select your color from the dropdown menu.

If you ever highlight text and want to remove the highlight, you can do so by selecting that text, going to the highlight dropdown, and choosing the "no color" option.

Once you've used the highlighter it will show the last color you used as the default color until you close the file. (This carries across documents. I have three documents open at the moment and all three of them now show "no color" as the highlighter option even though I only used it in the one document.)

BOLDING TEXT

This is one you will use often. At least I do. The easiest way to bold text is to use Ctrl + B. You can use it before you start typing the text you want to bold or on a selection of text that you've chosen. For text that is already bolded, you can remove the bolding by selecting the text and using Ctrl + B as well. If you select text that is both bolded and not bolded, you'll need to type Ctrl + B twice, once to bold all of the text and once to remove it.

If you don't want to use the control keys, you can also go to the Font Section of the Home tab and click on the B on the left-hand side. It works the exact same way as using Ctrl + B. If you click on it and then type text that text will be bolded. Or you can select the text you want to bold and then click on the B. To turn off or remove bolding, click on the B again.

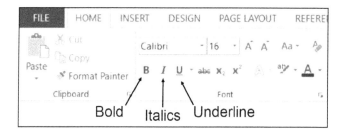

The final option is to select your text, right-click, choose Font from the dropdown menu, and then choose to Bold in the Font Style section of the Font dialogue box. (If you want to both bold and italicize text, you would choose Bold Italic.)

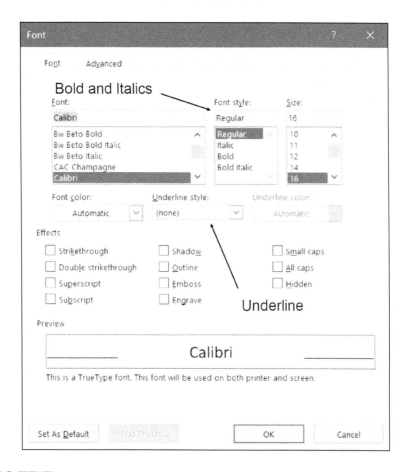

ITALICIZING TEXT

To place text into italics—that means to have it sloped to the side *like this*—the easiest way is to use Ctrl + I. It works the exact same way as bolding text. You can do it before you type the letters or select the text and then use it. And to remove italics, just select the text, and then type Ctrl + I until the italics are gone.

Or in the Font section of the Home tab, you can click on the slanted capital I. And if you use the Font dialogue box, italics are listed under Font Styles. (See the images above in the Bolding section.)

UNDERLINING TEXT

Underlining text works much the same way as bolding or italicizing text. The control keys you'll need to use are Ctrl + U and in the Font section of the Home tab the underline option is represented by an underlined U. (See image above in the Bolding section.)

Underline is different from italics and bold, though, because there are multiple underline options to choose from. Using Ctrl + U will provide a single line underline of your text. So will just clicking on the U in the Font section of the Home tab.

But if you click on the arrow next to the U in the Font section, you will see seven additional underline options you can choose from.

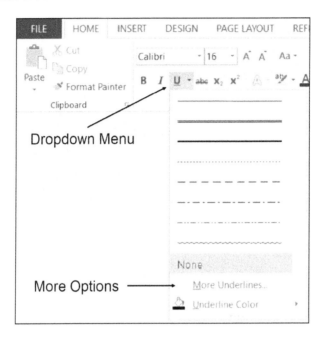

Choosing More Underlines at the bottom of that list of options will open the Font dialogue box where you will have a total of seventeen underline styles to choose from. You can also go direct to the Font dialogue box by selecting your text and then right-clicking and choosing Font from the dropdown. But, honestly, while it's good to know those other options are there the basic single underline will be all you need most of the time so if you remember anything remember Ctrl +U.

REMOVING BOLDING, UNDERLINING, OR ITALICS

I touched on this briefly above, but let's go over it again.

If you have bolded, underlined, or italicized text and you want to remove that formatting, you can simply select the text and use the command in question to remove that formatting type. So Ctrl + B, I, or U or click on the letter in the Font section of the Home tab or go to the Font dialogue box and remove the formatting from there.

If you select text that is partially formatted one way and partially formatted another—so say half of it is bolded and half is not—you may need to use the command twice. The first time will apply the formatting to all of the selected text, the second time will remove it from all of the selected text.

Also, with specialty underlining (all but the default, first choice), using Ctrl + U once will revert the type of underlining to the basic single underline. To remove the underline altogether, you'll need to use Ctrl + U a second time.

COPYING FORMATTING

There are going to be times where you've already formatted part of your document or you have a document that's formatted in the way you want and you want to "copy" that formatting to another portion of your document or a different document. This is where the Format Painter tool comes in handy. It's located on the Home tab in the Clipboard section.

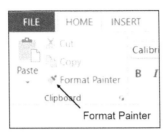

We have yet to discuss formatting paragraphs, but it's really useful when it comes to that because it will copy not only basic formatting like the font, font size, color, bolding, underline, italics, etc. but also the paragraph spacing and indent. Often in my corporate career I was able to use the format painter to fix a document when nothing else worked.

If you want to take formatting from one set of text and use it on another, first select the text with the formatting you want. Next, click on the Format Painter image. Finally, select the text you want to copy the formatting to.

A few tips.

You need to use the mouse or trackpad to select the text you want to have the formatting. Using the arrow and shift keys doesn't work.

You'll know that the format painter is ready to paint the format when you see a little paintbrush next to your cursor as you hover over your document.

You can sweep formatting that's in one document to another document.

Format painting can be unreliable if there are different formats in the sample you're taking the formatting from. For example, if I have a sample where part of the text is red and part of the text is bolded and I format sweep from that sample to new text, only the formatting of the first letter in my sample will carry over.

Sometimes with paragraph or numbered list formatting, I have to select the paragraph from the bottom to the top instead of top to bottom in order to get the format painter to carry over the formatting I want. And sometimes I need to select more than one paragraph to sweep from in order to get the line spacing to carry over.

Last but not least, when you copy formatting over, all of the formatting in your target text will be removed. This can be an issue if you've used italics or bolding within a paragraph, for example. Maybe you want the paragraph spacing and font and font size from another document so you use the format painter. Problem is, any bold, italics, or underline in the text you're copying the formatting to will be lost.

We'll talk about how to do this later, but there is a way in newer versions of Word to find all italicized text in a document. Same with bolded or underlined. So you could format sweep and then go back to a prior version of the document, locate the italics, bolding, and underlining, and manually put them back into the document now that it has the new formatting. It all depends on which option will be easier.

In summary, while the format painter is incredibly powerful and I use it all the time, you also need to be cautious in how you apply it so that you don't inadvertently introduce errors or erase formatting you don't want to erase. Sometimes it's the only way I can get paragraphs to look the same. Nothing else will do it. So learn this tool. It *will* save you at some point or another.

PARAGRAPH FORMATTING

That was basic text formatting. Now it's time to cover paragraph formatting. This is where you set the indent for a paragraph or make sure that it's double-spaced or that there's enough separation between paragraphs.

In this guide we're going to walk through how to change the formatting of a specific paragraph. Once you're comfortable enough in Word, I'd advise that you learn Styles and use those instead. We're not going to cover them in this guide because to really use them well you need to create customized Styles which is beyond a beginner-level skill. I will touch on a few points about Styles at the end of this chapter, though, and they are covered in *Intermediate Word* if you reach the point you want to learn about them. (Also, at the end of this guide I'll point you towards other resources you can use to learn what isn't covered here.)

Alright then. Let's talk about how to format a paragraph one element at a time.

PARAGRAPH ALIGNMENT

There are four choices for paragraph alignment. Left, Center, Right, and Justified. In the image below I've taken the same three-line paragraph and applied each alignment style to it:

This paragraph is **left-aligned**. I now need to add enough text to this paragraph to make more than one line so you can see the difference between the different alignments. Good times. Especially since I need at least three lines each for you to really see this.

This paragraph is **centered**. I now need to add enough text to this paragraph to make more than one line so you can see the difference between the different alignments. Good times. Especially since I need at least three lines each for you to really see this.

This paragraph is **right-aligned**. I now need to add enough text to this paragraph to make more than one line so you can see the difference between the different alignments. Good times. Especially since I need at least three lines each for you to really see this.

This paragraph is **justified**. I now need to add enough text to this paragraph to make more than one line so you can see the difference between the different alignments. Good times. Especially since I need at least three lines each for you to really see this.

Left-aligned, the first example, is how you'll often see text in documents. The text is lined up along the left-hand side of the page and allowed to end in a jagged line on the right-hand side of the page.

Justified, the last example, is the other common way for text to be presented. Text is still aligned along the left-hand side, but instead of leaving the right-hand side ragged, Word adjusts the spacing between words so that all lines are also aligned along the right-hand side.

For school papers and most work documents you're probably going to use left-alignment. Some places may prefer justified. Books are often published with justified but many do use left-aligned.

Centered, the second example, is rarely used for full paragraphs of text like the main body text of a book. It can be used for sections of text that are only a few lines long such as a quote that starts a chapter. Also, it's often used for chapter or section titles that are then centered over left-aligned or justified text. As you can see, it centers each line and distributes the text for that line equally to the left and right of the center point.

Right-aligned, the third example, is rare. It aligns all of the text along the right-hand side and leaves the left-hand side ragged. I have seen it used for text in side margins of non-fiction books and would expect to see it used for languages that read right to left.

Now that you understand the difference between the options, how do you change the paragraph alignment of your text? As with font, you can do this either before you start typing or by selecting text you've already typed. (For just one paragraph, you can click anywhere in the paragraph, you don't need to select the whole paragraph.)

The way I change paragraph alignment is by going to the Paragraph section of the Home tab and clicking on the image for the alignment type I need in the bottom row of that section.

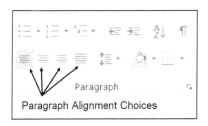

Paragraph Alignment Choices

Each image contains lines that show that type of alignment, but you can also hold your mouse over each one and Word will tell you which one it is.

There are also control shortcuts. Ctrl + L will left-align, Ctrl + E will center your text, Ctrl + R will right-align, and Ctrl + J will justify it. The only one of these I use enough to have memorized is Ctrl + E. I either use left-alignment, which is the default, or I use a Style that includes justifying the text. Since centering is something you do with section headers, I do use that one fairly often.

The third way to change your paragraph alignment is to right-click in your document and choose Paragraph from the dropdown menu. This will give you the Paragraph dialogue box. The first option within that box is a dropdown where you can choose the alignment type you want.

PARAGRAPH SPACING

If you've ever attended school in the United States, you've probably been told at some point to submit a five-page paper that's double-spaced with one inch margins. Or if you've ever submitted a short story you were told to use a specific line spacing. So how do you do that?

As with the other formatting options, you can either do this before you start typing or by selecting the paragraphs you want to change after they've been entered into the document.

Once you're ready, go to the Paragraph section of the Home tab and locate the Line and Paragraph Spacing option. It's to the right of the paragraph alignment options and looks like five lines of text with two big blue arrows on the left-hand side, one pointing up, one pointing down. Click on the small black arrow to the right of the image to bring up the dropdown menu.

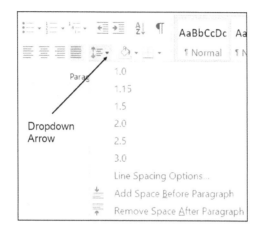

You'll see that you have a choice of single-spaced (1.0) or double-spaced (2.0) as well as 1.15, 1.5, 2.5, and 3.0 spacing. If you want a different spacing than one of those options, then click on Line Spacing Options at the bottom of the list to bring up the Paragraph dialogue box. There you can enter an exact number or choose from even more options. Generally, the dropdown will be sufficient, though.

Another option, of course, is to just go straight to the Paragraph dialogue box by right-clicking and choosing Paragraph from the dropdown menu. (Just remember to have already selected the text you want to change or to change the spacing before you start typing.)

BULLETED LISTS

A bulleted list is just what it sounds like, a list of items where each line starts with a bullet mark on the left-hand side. The most common bullet choice is probably a small dark black circle that's filled in, but Word has a few options you can choose from:

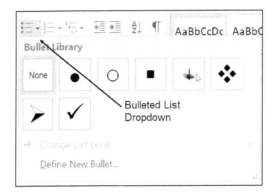

To create a bulleted list, go to the Paragraph section of the Home tab and click on the bulleted list dropdown menu to select the type of bullet you want to use in your list.

If you know that what you're about to type is going to be a bulleted list, you can click on the bulleted list option before you start typing. Word will insert the bullet you've chosen and move the cursor to where your text will start.

If you've already typed the first row of text that you want bulleted, you can click on the bulleted list option you want while in that row of text and it will convert it to the first entry of a bulleted list.

Hitting enter at the end of the line in a bulleted list, will start a new line with a bullet.

Or, last but not least, if all of your text has already been entered you can select all of the lines that you want to be part of the bulleted list and then choose the bulleted list option and it should convert your text to a bulleted list with one bullet per paragraph or individual line.

If you have a line that's bulleted and you don't want it to be, you can go to the beginning of the text on that line and backspace. Once will remove the bullet. Twice will move the text to the beginning of the line. Or, you can select the line and choose None from the bulleted list dropdown menu.

(You can also use the Format Painter to apply bullets to a list of entries or to remove them depending on the formatting of your source data.)

Another way to create a bulleted list is to select your text and then right-click to bring up the mini formatting menu. The bulleted list dropdown is one of the available options.

With bulleted lists, Word automatically indents your text. If you don't want that, you can use the Decrease Indent option (discussed below) to move the text back to the left-hand side of the page but keep the bullets.

NUMBERED LISTS

You can also create a "numbered" list that uses letters or numbers for each entry in your list instead of bullets.

One easy way to create a numbered list in more recent versions of Word is to simply type the first number you want to use, the separator mark you want, and then a space. Word will automatically indent that entry and turn it into the first entry in a numbered list. So, for example, I might type the number 1 followed by a period and then a space. Word will indent that 1. and make it the first entry in my list. This works with all of the options on the dropdown menu we're about to look at. (This is part of the Autocorrect settings, so a little thunderbolt will appear next to the number when this first happens. If you don't want that to happen, you can click on the arrow next to the thunderbolt and have Word reverse the change by telling it to Undo Automatic Numbering.)

When you hit enter after typing in the text for your first line, Word will continue the numbering you started.

The other option, especially if you already have your list and just need to convert it to a numbered list, is to select the lines you want to number, go to the Home tab and in the Paragraph section click on the arrow next to the Numbering option and choose the numbered list option you want from there.

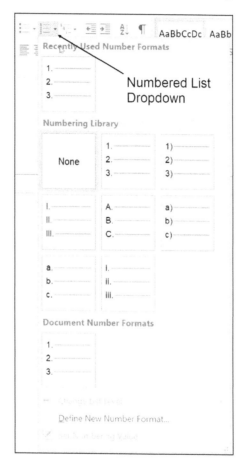

As you can see, you have the option to choose between lists that use 1, 2, 3 or i, ii, iii or A, B, C or a, b, c, or I, II, III and then between using a period after the "number" or a paren. For a basic list, this should be all you really need.

When you right-click on your list you'll also see that the mini formatting menu is available and that one of the options is the numbering option. So instead of going to the Home tab, you could just right-click and choose from there to create your numbered list.

You can also create two-level or three-level lists by using the tab key to indent your numbering or the shift-tab key to decrease the indent on your numbering. This gives you, for example, a first level that is 1, 2, 3 with the option of a second level under that that's a, b, c. To do this, go to each line you want to be second-level (or third-level) and use the tab key to indent that line. This will change the numbering of the line at the same time it moves it inward.

If you need very fine control over a multi-level list or you need a list that works throughout your document and has lots of breaks in it, you'll probably want to use an option we're not going to cover here called the Multilevel List option. (It's the option to the right of the number list option in the Paragraph section.) I discuss that option in *Intermediate Word*, but I'll tell you now that it's incredibly finicky to use and one of the things I hate most in Word.

Back to basic numbered lists. If you had a numbered list earlier in your document and want that numbering to continue in the location where you are now, you can do that. Or, if Word continued the numbering and you wanted it to start over at 1, you can do that, too. In either case, you're going to right-click on the number you want to change. You'll then either choose Continue Numbering (to continue from a prior section) or Set Numbering Value (to change the value you start with back to 1 or A or whatever you're using).

INDENTING AN ENTIRE PARAGRAPH OR LIST

Now that we've talked about lists, let's talk about increasing or decreasing an indent. When you're dealing with paragraphs, the best way to do this is in the Paragraph dialogue box. Right-click on your paragraph and from the dropdown menu choose Paragraph. Once the Paragraph dialogue box opens, you can set the indent for the entire paragraph as well as whether the paragraph will have a special indent only for the first line.

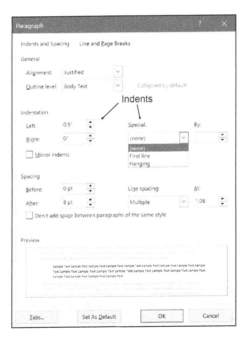

To indent the entire paragraph, change the value under Indentation where it says Left. To indent just the first line of a paragraph, choose First Line from the dropdown menu under Special and then select by how much in the By box. To have the first line flush left, but the lines below that indented, choose Hanging from the dropdown menu under Special and then selected how much those other lines should be indented by entering a value in the By box. (Usually .3 is a good value to go with, Word defaults to .5)

If you just want to indent a line of text or an entire paragraph, you can use the Increase Indent (or Decrease Indent) options in the Paragraph section of the Home tab. These are the ones that have four lines with blue arrows pointing either to the left (for decrease indent) or the right (for increase indent). You can also use tab (to indent) and shift + tab (to decrease an indent).

The problem with the increase indent/decrease indent menu options or the tab keys is in how Word records this for your paragraph format. For example, I just took a single word and indented it using the tab key. Word interpreted this as me wanting that paragraph to be formatted as having a First Line indent of .5". When I instead used the increase indent option on that single word of text, Word interpreted it as Left Indentation of .5". If it's just one line of text, it doesn't matter. But when you're dealing with an entire document, these little discrepancies can become a nightmare.

For bulleted and numbered lists, if you want to move an entire list further to the right or further to the left, select the entire list and then use either the Paragraph dialogue box, the shift or shift + tab keys, or the increase or decrease indent options from the Paragraph section of the Home tab to move it. The Paragraph dialogue box will give you the most control. The tab and shift + tab keys are probably the easiest to use. You can also right-click and choose Adjust Line Indents.

(If you choose Adjust Line Indents, you can also adjust the space between the number and the text by changing the Follow Number With option. This can be very useful when you have a numbered list that gets into the double digits.)

SPACING BETWEEN PARAGRAPHS

If you choose to style your paragraphs as left-aligned with no first line indent, you're going to need space between your paragraphs. The default style in Word is set up this way. You'll see that as you hit enter for a new paragraph that there's space left between the old paragraph and the new one.

If that space isn't present, you may be tempted to create one by using the enter key. Don't. It will mess with your formatting in a larger document as those spaces you've entered end up at the top or bottom of your pages. It's better to instead format your paragraphs to include the space.

You can do this by selecting your paragraph(s) and going to the Paragraph section of the Home tab. Click on the arrow next to the Line and Paragraph Spacing image (the lines with two blue arrows on the left-hand side, one pointing upward, one pointing downward), and choose Add Space Before Paragraph. In my version of Word that adds a 12 point space before the selected paragraphs.

If you want more control over the spacing around your paragraphs, right-click in your document and choose Paragraph to bring up the Paragraph dialogue box. The third section of the Indent and Spacing tab covers Spacing. On the left side you can see options for Before and After with arrows up and down. You can either type in a spacing value or you can use the arrows to choose the value you want.

If you set your paragraphs to have spacing both before and after, the space between two paragraphs will be the higher of those two values not the combination of them. (So if you say 12 point before and 6 point after, the spacing between them will be 12 point not 18 point.)

If you just wanted spacing at the top of a section of paragraphs or at the bottom of a section of paragraphs, you can click the box to say don't add spacing to paragraphs of the same style. Or just add paragraph spacing to that top-most or bottom-most paragraph. Usually this will come into play when you're dealing with a numbered list and want to separate it from the paragraphs of text above and below, but don't want that separation within your list.

If you don't want a space that is there, you can choose Remove Space After Paragraph from the dropdown in the Paragraph section of the Home tab. If you use this method, just be sure you've selected the correct paragraph (the one before the space you want to remove). Or, you can open the Paragraph dialogue box and change the paragraph spacing values for before and after to zero.

(Paragraph spacing is one of those issues that can become a nightmare in a large document where multiple users have been making edits. This is where sometimes using Format Painter to get the spacing between paragraphs consistent can be a lifesaver.)

OTHER FUNCTIONS

We've talked about how to enter text into Word and how to format that text once you've entered it and how to format your paragraphs. But there are a few more basics we need to cover that don't really have anything to do with entering or formatting your text, although they may lead to changes in your text.

Let's start with Find and Replace.

FIND

If you want to find a particular word or phrase in a Word document and you don't want to scan through the whole document, you'll need to use Find. It's very easy.

There are a few ways to do it (as is the case with most of the older functions in Word).

First, you can type Ctrl + F. In earlier versions of Word this would've brought up the Find and Replace dialogue box. In newer versions of Word this may instead just take your cursor to the Navigation search box on the left-hand side of the screen. If all you're looking for is a simple word or phrase, type it into the search box.

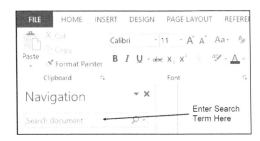

(Depending on how your document is set up, that search box may already be there for you to use. It is in my current document.)

Once you type a word into the search document box, Word will highlight that word or phrase throughout your document and tell you just below the search box how many total results there were. You can either scan through the document for all highlights of your search term or use the arrows next to the number of results to find the matches.

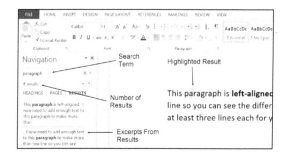

If you click on RESULTS directly under the search box, Word will show you a small snippet of each result on the left-hand side of the screen. In larger documents when you're looking for a very specific usage, scanning the results list can save time. For example, in this document when I just searched for "word" there were 92 matches. It's easier to look at the results list than scan through a thirty page document to look at each highlighted result.

To close your search, just click on the X next to the search term or hit Esc.

Another way to initiate Find is to go to the Editing section of the Home tab (on the far right) and click on Find from there.

But Find is more powerful than this basic search. You can do an Advanced Find that searches by formatting or limits your search results based on various criteria. To do that, you need to bring up the Find and Replace dialogue box.

One way to do so is to go to the Editing Section of the Home tab and click on the small black arrow next to Find. From the dropdown menu select Advanced Find. (Another way to do so is to type Ctrl +H and then click on the Find tab of the Find and Replace dialogue box.)

At first the Find tab doesn't look much more interesting than a basic search. That is until you click on the More option at the bottom left corner, which brings up a number of different search options.

Two of the most important options I use are "Match Case" and "Find Whole Words Only".

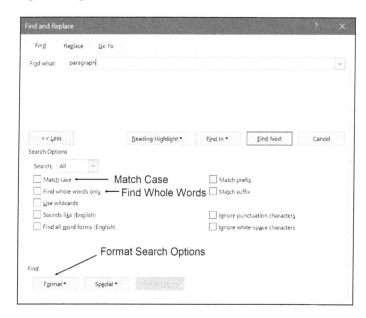

Match Case will look at the search term you enter and only find words with the same capitalization. So if you search for "CAT" and you check this box it will only locate "CAT" for you. If you didn't check this box, it would also locate "cat". (In this case CAT stands for consolidated audit trail and cat is an animal.) When searching for a proper name or an abbreviation like that, I recommend always checking this box.

Find Whole Words Only will only search for the entire word you enter. So again, with the example of "CAT", if you just searched Word normally it would return any word that has "cat" in it. So "category" and "implication" would be returned along with "CAT" and "cat."

Using Match Case and Find Whole Words saves you time when used with Find, but they can be vitally important when used with Replace.

Those are the only two options I use of the ones listed in that section. I can envision how some of the others would be useful, but I've ever needed them in twenty-plus years of using Word. What I have used is the Format option in the bottom left corner. If you click on that it will bring up a dropdown menu of options. One of them is Font.

Clicking on Font will bring up a Find Font dialogue box where you can specify the formatting you want to search for. In the screenshot below, I've chosen to find all text in italics. You can see it selected in the Find Font dialogue box and after I clicked on OK it was added under my search term.

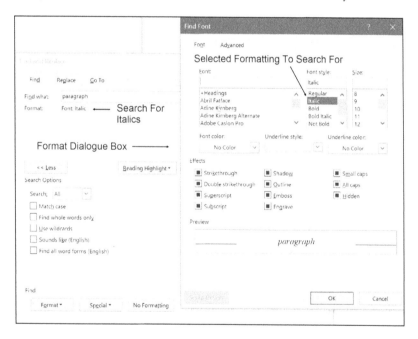

To find all italic text in the document, leave the search term box blank. When you click on search Word will show you all of the italic text in your document. This works for any type of formatting you want to find in your document and is good for combinations of formatting.

If all you want is to find text in italics (or text that's bolded or underlined), another way to do this is to click into the search box and then use the control key shortcuts. Typing Ctrl + I once will change the search so that you're looking for italicized text. Typing it another time will change the search so that you're looking for text that isn't in italics. Typing it a third time will remove it from the search.

Be careful when using the formatting search options that you don't forget to change an option and end up missing a search result you wanted to see. (For example, leaving it with no italics when you want all instances of a certain word, even those in italics.)

One last point. If you click on Special at the bottom of the Find and Replace dialogue box you'll see a list of special characters or attributes that you can also search on such as tabs and em dashes.

REPLACE

Find is useful. Replace is fantastic.

I have a bad habit with my novels of deciding after the novel is written that a character name needs to be changed. For example, I had a 90,000-word novel with a medic whose name was Marian. After reading Medic Marian one too many times I decided she needed a new name. But manually changing it would've been a nightmare. Find and Replace took care of it in less than a minute.

Same with fixing two spaces after a period. That's how I was taught to do things in school, so it's instinct by now. But there's a lot of negativity towards using two spaces after a period in the writing community, so now when I finish writing a piece I use find and replace to replace all instances of two spaces with one. I get to type the way I'm used to and I also get to deprive those judgey judgey types an opportunity to be nasty. Win win.

Having said that…

It's easy to mess up find and replace. Usually by not thinking through the implications of the changes you're going to make. Like in the example we had above with CAT. Let's say your boss wants you to replace all uses of CAT with consolidated audit trail. So you do. You do a quick find and replace for CAT and think you're done. Problem is, if you didn't think this through and use Find Whole Words Only and Match Case you also just replaced the "cat" in implication with "consolidated audit trail." Now you have a place somewhere in your document that reads "impliconsolidated audit trailion." Hopefully you'd catch that in spellcheck. But you wouldn't catch an instance where you replaced "cat", meaning the animal, with consolidated audit trail. You'd have some very confused readers when they reached the point where the firemen rescued the consolidated audit trail from the tree.

(I know. That's ridiculous and would never happen. But other things like that have happened.) Not what you want.

So the basics. To find text (or formatting) in your document and replace it, you can use Ctrl + H to bring up the Find and Replace dialogue box or you can go to the Editing section of the Home tab and click on Replace.

What you'll see is a Find What box and a Replace With box. In the Find What box type what you want to find. In the Replace With box type what you want to replace it with. So when I'm hunting down double spaces after a period I click into the Find What box and type two spaces and then click into the Replace With box and type a single space. Next, I click on Replace All and Word replaces all of the two spaces in the document and tells me how many replacements it made.

If you want to be more careful about what you're replacing, you can instead click on Replace. Word will locate the next instance of what you told it to find and highlight it. Click Replace again to replace the text that's highlighted with what you told it to use for the replacement. Word will do so and then go on to the next instance. If you don't want to replace that one, click on Find Next until you do find an instance you want to replace. When you do, click on Replace.

As with Find, you have the More option that lets you find whole words, match the case of your search term, and search by formatting.

Here's an example of a find/replace where I'm looking for instances of "paragraph" that aren't in italics and replacing them with "paragraph" in italics.

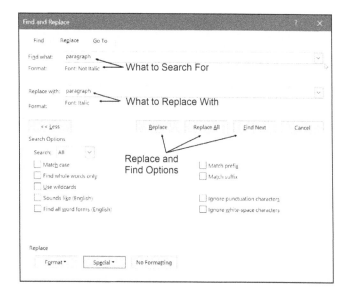

One other item to note. When Word does the find and replace, it will sometimes do so only from where you are in the document forward. When this happens it tells you how many items it found and replaced and then asks if you want to continue searching from the beginning. To be sure that you've found all instances, say yes.

SPELLING AND GRAMMAR CHECK

Unless you've done something to your settings or are working in a document that's already hundreds of pages long, you'll notice little red and blue squiggly lines appear under some words as you type. This is Word's real-time spelling and grammar check at work.

> As with Find, you can also fine-tune your search by clicking on <u>More</u>. This is where Match Case and Find Whole Words Only are incredibly powerful. No accidentally replacing all instances of "tom" with "bill" including changing "tomorrow" into "<u>billorrow</u>".

In the image above, there's a red squiggly line under "billorow" because that's not a real word, so Word identified it as a misspelling. The blue squiggly line under "More" is there because Word thinks that's a potential grammar error since I have a word capitalized in the middle of a sentence.

For spelling errors, you can right-click on the word and Word will suggest possible spellings if you're close enough to the actual spelling for it to guess the word. For grammar errors, it'll suggest the fix as well, but I usually leave those until the end when I run Spelling and Grammar check on the entire document.

The Spelling & Grammar check can be found in the Review tab on the left side in the Proofing section.

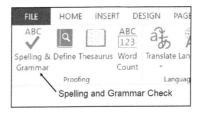

Once you click on it, Word will walk its way through your entire document checking for spelling and grammar issues. When it finds one it will display on the right side of the screen the issue it found and what it suggests as possible ways to fix it. You can ignore the suggestion, agree to the suggestion (by clicking on Change), or click into the document and type in your own edit to fix the issue.

With spelling errors, you can also choose to Ignore All if this is a word that's used repeatedly throughout the document but is not an error. (Like a made-up name or industry abbreviation.) In the alternative, you can choose to Change All if you think this is an error you've made more than once and you trust that there's never a time the word was used that doesn't need changed.

As you can see below, with spelling errors sometimes Word gives you multiple alternative words to choose from. Be sure you click on the correct one before selecting Change.

A word of caution when using the spelling and grammar check: Word is very good with spelling errors. It's not so good with grammar issues. More than once it has suggested the wrong version of its and it's to me. And it often fails to parse complex sentences properly, so ends up suggesting me instead of I when it shouldn't. You can read the explanations it gives, but don't assume that just because Word flagged a potential grammar error that it's right. Do not use it blindly. You will introduce errors into your document if you do.

When Word finishes with the spelling and grammar check it will display a Readability Statistics dialogue box. I sometimes find it interesting to know what grade level I've written to, but it's mostly useless for day-to-day purposes. Just close it out.

Also, once you've run spellcheck on a document and told Word to ignore spelling or grammar errors, it will continue to do so in that document. To run a clean spelling and grammar check of your document, go to the File tab and click on Options. Next, click on Proofing and click on the gray box labeled Recheck Document. This will show you a notice that you're about to reset the spelling and grammar check. Click OK. Now when you look at the document all spelling and grammar errors will be shown once more and when you run the spelling and grammar check it will show you everything it considers a spelling or grammar error.

WORD COUNT

One piece of information that can be useful in that Readability Statistics dialogue box is the word count of your document. Some short story markets, for example, have word count limits and some online forms restrict you to a certain number of characters. To see how many characters or words are in your document (or in a selection from your document), go to the Proofing section of the Review tab and choose Word Count. You'll now see the Word Count dialogue box which tells you the number of words, number of characters, and number of characters without spaces for your document or selection.

Your current word count is also usually visible in the bottom left corner of your document.

PAGE FORMATTING

We talked about how to format individual text and how to format paragraphs, but we still need to cover how to format a page. This is more relevant for when you want to print a document, which is why I saved it until this point.

PAGE NUMBERING

If you're going to print your document, you'll likely want to number the pages in the document. DO NOT do this manually. Word will do this for you and by letting Word do this, you ensure that the page numbering isn't changed when you make edits to the document.

To add page numbers to your document, go to the Header & Footer section of the Insert tab and click on the arrow next to Page Number. This will bring up a dropdown menu that lets you choose where on the page you want your page numbers to display and then how you want those page numbers to look.

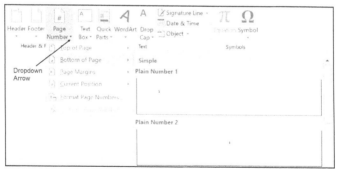

That should be all you need. Go there, choose Bottom of Page, Plain Number 2, and you'll have a document that has a page number centered at the bottom of each page.

In *Intermediate Word* I talk about how to create section breaks so that you have different page numbering in different parts of your document, but for basic, simple, page numbering you don't need to do more than I just showed you.

HEADERS AND FOOTERS

If you want text to repeat at the top or bottom of every page, then you should use headers and footers. Again, don't try to manually put this information into your document. One little change to your text and it'll break. (Not to mention how it'll look on an ereader.)

A header goes at the top of your page.

A footer goes at the bottom of your page.

To add one, go to the Header & Footer section of the Insert tab and click on the arrow below the one you need (header or footer), and then choose the option that works best for you, just like you did with page numbering.

You're not stuck with the format you choose. For example, with short story submissions, they usually want the header to be in the top right corner. If you choose the Blank header option, that creates a header that's in the top left corner. But you can simply go to the Home tab and choose to right-align the text in your header and that will put it in the right corner instead.

After you choose your header or footer option, Word inserts [Type here] into the designated spots where you're supposed to put text. To edit this text, just start typing because it will already be highlighted in gray. If it isn't, select the text and then start typing. Text in your header or footer works just like text in your document. You can use the same options from the Home tab to change your font, font size, color, etc.

Headers and footers are in a separate area from the main text of your document. So if you're in a header or footer and want to go back to the main document, you can (1) click on Close Header and Footer in the menu bar, (2) hit the Esc key on your keyboard, or (3) double-click on the main text in your document which will be grayed out while you're in the header or footer.

If you're in your main document and want to open a header or footer, you can (1) double-click on the text in the header or footer, or (2) right-click on the header or footer and choose "Edit Header" or "Edit Footer" from the dropdown options. I've found in recent versions of Word that double-clicking when there's just a page number in the footer doesn't work well for me and that I have to right-click and choose Edit Footer instead. This was not true of older versions of Word.

MARGINS

Margins are the white space along the edges of your document. The default in my version of Word is one-inch margins all around which is what most submission guidelines I've seen require, so you usually won't need to edit these. But in case you do...

(Because it looks like at least in Word 2003 the margins were not one inch all around.)

Go to the Page Layout tab and under the Page Setup section click on the dropdown under Margins. You will see some standard choices to choose from or the option at the bottom to set custom margins. If you click on Custom Margins, it will take you to the Page Setup dialogue box where you can specify the margins for top, bottom, left, and right.

You can also open the Page Setup dialogue box directly by clicking on the expansion arrow for the Page Setup section.

PAGE ORIENTATION

A standard document has a page orientation of portrait. That's where the long edge of the document is along the sides and the short edge is across the bottom and top. This is how most books, business reports, and school papers are formatted, and it's the default in Word.

But sometimes you'll create a document where you need to turn the text ninety degrees so that the long edge is at the top and bottom and the short edge is on the sides. A lot of tables in appendixes are done this way. And presentation slides are often this way. That's called landscape orientation.

(Think paintings here. A drawing of a person—a portrait—is taller than it is wide. A drawing of a mountain range—a landscape—is wider than it is tall.)

To change the orientation of your document, go to the Page Setup section of the Page Layout tab, click on the arrow under Orientation, and choose the orientation you want.

(If you use section breaks--which are covered in *Intermediate Word*—you can set the page orientation on a section-by-section basis. But if you're not using sections changing the orientation on any page will change the orientation of the entire document.)

PRINTING

Printing in Word, at its most basic, is incredibly easy. You can simply type Ctrl + P or go to File and choose Print from the list of options on the left-hand side. Both options will bring you to the Print screen.

On the right-hand side you can see what the document will look like when it prints. For documents that are longer than a page, you can use the arrows at the bottom to navigate through the document preview. If everything looks good, you can just click on the Print icon.

But there are some changes you can make at this stage, so let's walk through them.

COPIES

Right next to the Print icon you can specify the number of copies of the document you want to print. The default is one copy. To increase that amount, either type a new number into the box or use the arrows on the right-hand side.

PRINTER

Your default printer should already be showing under the printer option. Sometimes I will change this to print to Microsoft XPS Document Writer or, if I'm working on a corporate computer, a PDF. This is for when I don't want to print a physical copy of the document but would like to have a version that can't be easily edited. (You can also use Save As to create a PDF version.)

SETTINGS: PRINT ALL PAGES OR PAGES

Below the printer choice are all the Settings options. In the Print All Pages and Pages section just below it you can choose to print just a subset of the pages in your document. For example, sometimes I just want to print one section or one page of a document.

You can choose from the dropdown to print the current page, print text that you've selected (print selection), only print odd pages, or only print even pages.

In the Pages box you can list individual page numbers that you want to print. For page ranges, use a dash. For a list of individual pages, use commas. So if you want to print pages 3, 5, and 7 you would enter "3,5,7" in the Pages box. If you wanted to print pages 3 *through* 7, you would enter "3-7" in the box. When you enter a page range in the Pages box it changes the dropdown menu to "Custom Print."

SETTINGS: PRINT ONE-SIDED OR TWO-SIDED

The default is for Word to print on one side of the page, but you can change it to print two-sided documents. To do so, click on the arrow next to the default choice of one-sided. You'll now see a dropdown with four options, one-sided, both sides with the long edge, both sides with the short edge, and manually print on both sides.

Choose the manual option if you have a printer that isn't set up to print two-sided documents.

Choose to flip pages on the long edge for documents with a portrait orientation. (This will be most documents.) Choose to flip pages on the short edge for documents with a landscape orientation.

SETTINGS: COLLATION

This is only relevant if you're printing more than one copy of a document that's more than one page long.

The default when printing multiple copies of a document is to print one entire copy of the document and then print the next copy of the document. (That's the collated option that shows 1,2,3 and then 1,2,3.)

The other option you can choose is to print all of your page ones and then all of your page twos and then all of your page threes. (That's the uncollated option that shows 1,1,1 and 2,2,2, etc.) The uncollated option is useful for situations where you might be giving out handouts one page at a time, but generally you'll want to stick with collated copies.

SETTINGS: ORIENTATION

We talked about this one before, but if you want the text on your page to go across the long edge instead of the short edge, this is another place where you can make that selection. The default is Portrait Orientation, but if you click on the arrow, you can instead choose Landscape Orientation.

SETTINGS: PAPER SIZE

The default in Word (at least in the U.S. version) is to print on 8.5"x11" paper. If you want to print your document on a different size of paper (say A4 or legal), then this is where you'd change that setting.

There are an insane number of choices both on the dropdown menu and if you click on More Paper Sizes but for most documents you'll probably be using the default.

If you do change the paper size, make sure that your printer has the correct paper in it.

SETTINGS: MARGINS

We already talked about how to change the margins on your document, but this is another place where you can do that. You have a list of pre-formatted options as well as the ability to customize.

SETTINGS: PAGES TO PRINT PER SHEET

If you want to save paper because perhaps you're reviewing a document and it's not the final version, you can print more than one page of your document onto a single sheet.

The default is to print one page on one sheet, but if you click on the dropdown menu here you can choose to print 2, 4, 6, 8, or 16 pages per sheet. You can also choose to scale your text to a chosen paper size.

Be careful with this, because Word will let you make a choice that results in an illegible document. Four pages on one is still legible, but I suspect that sixteen pages on one page would be virtually useless. (Unless you're in a situation where your teacher said you could bring one page of notes and you're trying to cram an entire semester's worth of knowledge on that one page.)

PAGE SETUP

As a beginner, I'd ignore the Page Setup link at the bottom of the page. Most of what it covers we've already addressed above. It's just the older way of specifying your print settings.

CUSTOMIZED SETTINGS

We're almost done, but before we wrap up I want to talk about how to customize your version of Word. I've already mentioned the Quick Access Toolbar, but there are some other settings I routinely adjust in order to get Word to work for me in the way I want it to.

Everything we're going to talk about in this section can be found in the File tab under Options with the exception of the last one which is found in the File tab under Info.

So first go to the File tab and from there click on Options. This will bring up the Word Options dialogue box (below).

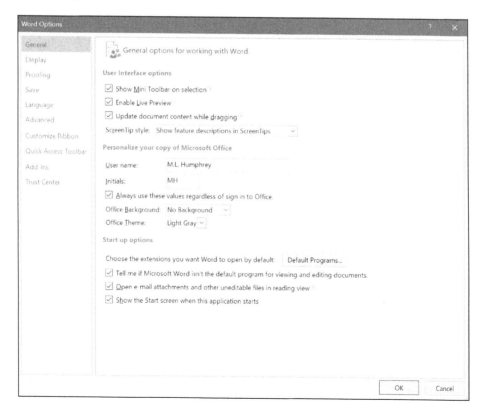

If there's a setting in Word that's giving you problems, chances are the way to fix it is buried somewhere in this dialogue box. I'll walk you through a few key things I change, but you might find it worthwhile to explore on your own. Just be warned that any changes you make here will affect *all* of your Word documents, not just this one. So be careful.

(And if you're using someone else's version of Word and wondering why it looks so different, changes they've made here could very well be the reason.)

FILE -> OPTIONS -> GENERAL SETTINGS

This is where you can customize how your user name and initials will display for things like track changes, adding comments, and document properties. (None of which we've discussed so far but which you may run into if you're working on group documents.)

If you're going to change this, like I have, you also need to check the box that says to always use these values. If you don't, newer versions of Word that use your Windows login will override what you put here.

FILE -> OPTIONS -> DISPLAY

I'm pretty sure I've customized this one by clicking on the box that says to show white space between pages in print layout view. Without this box checked, you can't visually see page breaks in your document. One page of text rolls right into the next with just a thin gray line to indicate a page break. It's fine when you're dealing with longer pages of text or a report without breaks, but when you have very short chapters or sections, you can end up with three or four of them displayed on a single page. That annoys me, so I change it.

FILE -> OPTIONS -> PROOFING

This one I always have to mess with.

My former day job involves a lot of rule citations, where you write things like Rule 3070(c). Unfortunately for me, one of the proofing defaults in Word is to automatically convert (c) into the copyright sign. That's probably very handy for most of the population, but a complete pain for someone like me. So every time I get a new version of Word, I have to remove that one from the list of AutoCorrect Options.

In the other tabs in this section you'll find things like replacing straight quotes with smart quotes (which you're supposed to do for fiction writing). To get this one to actually change, you have to make that change in two tabs, the AutoFormat as You Type tab and the AutoFormat tab.

This is also the area of Word where I have a setting that converts typing two dashes in a row into an em-dash. (If you do this, you need to space after the next word to get the conversion to happen. And if the word is a contraction you actually need to space before the apostrophe to get it to convert. So dash, dash, word, space and you'll get –word but type dash, dash, word and you'll just have --word.)

A lot of the autocorrect options are very handy—I often type too fast and mistype "the" and Word always catches that for me—but do keep an eye out for "errors" you don't want fixed as you type.

It's probably a good idea to take a look through the tabs just to make sure there aren't any listed that you know you won't want to use.

This is also the section where you can create a Custom Dictionary if your company allows it. For example, my first name is always flagged by spellcheck. When I can, I add it to my custom dictionary so I don't get a spelling alert every time I send an email.

This is also where you can customize the settings for the spelling and grammar check. I usually use the default settings, but if you don't want to have Word flagging issues as you type, this is where you can turn that off.

FILE -> OPTIONS -> SAVE

In this section can specify how often Word saves a recovery version of your document. This can be a life saver if your computer or Word crash while you're working.

I always have autorecovery turned on even though it can be annoying. For some reason the CreateSpace templates take forever to save the autorecovery version. And the document freezes while it's doing it. But all it takes is losing something you were working on once to appreciate how important autorecovery can be.

You can specify here how often Word should save and where it should store that file. In newer versions of Word when Word crashes the next time it opens you'll be given the option of opening the recovered version and/or the last saved version.

If that doesn't happen, notice here where those files are saved. There's a chance that you may be able to go to that location and recover the file you need from there.

Best practice, though, is to make a habit of saving your files on a regular basis even if you're not done with them yet.

FILE -> OPTIONS -> ADVANCED

There are a ton of options in this section. I don't recall changing any of these in my own personal version of Word, but you might want to glance through to see if there's something you want to change. (And it's possible that I did change one of these a couple years ago and now just don't remember it. I'm used to Word working in a certain way and when it doesn't I usually go looking for a way to fix it or change it to what I'm familiar with. But with all the choices in File -> Options, you only need to change them once and then they're that way for that version of Word forever or until you change them back.)

FILE -> OPTIONS -> CUSTOMIZE RIBBON

If you want to get really fancy, you can customize the content of the tabs at the top of the screen. Say you want everything you think you'll use consolidated onto your Home tab or know you'll never need to use Styles and want to remove them, you can do it. However…

I would advise against this. Because your customization will only exist in your current version of Word. It won't exist on your IT guy's version. It won't exist on your best friend's. It won't exist on the version that everyone else is using when they answer questions on the internet. Which means once you do this, you're on your own. Other people won't be able to tell you where to go in your version of Word to make something happen.

And, the minute you upgrade to a new version of Word or start a new job, you'll be back to using the standard layout.

FILE -> OPTIONS -> QUICK ACCESS TOOLBAR

This is another location for you to customize what appears on the Quick Access Toolbar, and this one I do customize. I've added Select All, Breaks, and Format Painter here.

FILE -> INFO

If you go to the File tab and click on Info, there are a few more things you can do with respect to your document that you need to know about. I hesitate to tell you about this, because people using it have caused me more issues than I can tell you. But since it may come up and is useful to know about, I'm going to tell you. Just be careful with this one, please. I can't help you if you screw this up.

Okay.

So when you work on a file in Word it stores a bunch of information behind the scenes including who the author of the document was. Sometimes, when you're going to share a document with a client or someone outside of your group, you'll want to strip that information out of your document and anonymize it to the extent you can. And if you've used comments or track changes in your document, it's a very good idea to make sure those are all removed before you pass the document outside of your team. (No one needs to see that back and forth you had over that paragraph on page five.)

The way you review your document for information you might want to remove is by going to the Info section of the File tab and clicking on Check for Issues next to Inspect Document, and then choosing to Inspect Document. This will scan your document for all sorts of things like comments, personal information, embedded documents, collapsed headings, etc.

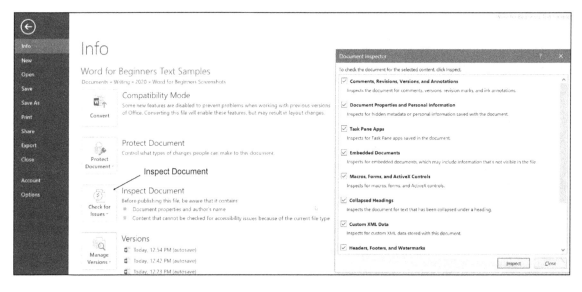

Some of this is very useful to check for. Some not so much. Like headers, footers, and watermarks. Chances are you wanted those in your document, so after you scan your document and Word offers to remove all of them, BE VERY CAREFUL. You can destroy a lot of work with just a click or two.

What I recommend if you're going to do this is that you save a copy of the file beforehand and then save the inspected and stripped down version as a new file. That way if you delete something you shouldn't, you can go back and fix it.

And always wait until the absolute end to strip out the personalization. I've been in situations where someone did this mid-review of a document and then everyone's comments on that document (and there were four or five of us providing comments) were listed as by Author. Believe it or not, that's a big deal. Because it matters whether that comment to edit something on page three was made by your boss or the new intern who doesn't know what they're doing but thinks they do.

So be careful. This one is useful but potentially dangerous.

CONCLUSION

Alright. There you have it. Enough knowledge about Word to let you do most of what you need to do. In *Intermediate Word* I dive into how to create complex numbered lists, insert tables, use section breaks, insert a table of contents, use styles, add watermarks and hyperlinks, deal with track changes, and more. Things that you may need to do at some point, but aren't essential.

If you found this guide easy to follow and want to learn that, then *Intermediate Word* is available for purchase. But there are other options. Now that you know the basics of Word, if you run into something you want to do but don't know how to do it, you can research how to do it either through Word or online.

First, within Word.

Hover your mouse over any of the options at the top of the screen and you'll see a basic description of what it does. For many of those options, at the bottom of the description is a question mark with the words Tell Me More. If you click on those words, you'll be taken to Word's built-in help function.

You can also click on the question mark in the top right corner of Word to bring up Word's built-in help function and then search for what you need to know.

I'll tell you, though. Nine times out of ten I search the help function in Word and give up after about a minute because what it says is nowhere close to what I need to know. But I always start there, just in case.

Usually, I end up doing an internet search for what I'm looking for using "microsoft word" as part of my search string. So I might search for "how to add a hyperlink microsoft word."

I then click on the result with the web address support.microsoft.com.

Bizarre as it is, given the general worthlessness of the built-in help function, the help provided on the Microsoft website is actually very good. If you want to know how something works, the website will almost always provide the information you need.

But it doesn't work so well with the "can I do X" sort of questions. (This is more often a problem with Excel than Word because there's only so much you can do in Word and it's mostly functional.)

If I have a "can I do X" sort of question, I do the exact same internet search as above, but instead of expecting an answer from Microsoft, I read through the top handful of results to see if anyone has asked my question before on a public forum and had it answered. Usually someone has.

If you still can't figure it out at that point (or even before that), you can also email me at mlhumphreywriter@gmail.com. I'm happy to point you in the right direction or figure out the answer myself. I don't check that email address every day, so you may have to wait a few days for me to get back to you, but I will get back to you eventually.

If all else fails, there are forums both on the Microsoft website and elsewhere where you can ask your question. Just be prepared for someone to imply that you're foolish or stupid for asking. I don't know why those types of forums are so obnoxious, but they are. It takes a bit of a thick skin to wade through and get the answer you need. Also, if you go that route, don't click on links from strangers. And be wary of anything that has you messing around in restricted files on your computer. It might work, it might break your computer.

Okay. So that's it. You should know the basics of Word at this point, and you now have the tools to find more answers if you need them. Good luck with it!

INDEX

CONTROL SHORTCUTS

For each of the control shortcuts, hold down Ctrl and the key listed to perform the command.

Command	Ctrl +
Select All	A
Bold	B
Copy	C
Center	E
Find	F
Replace	H
Italicize	I
Print	P
Save	S
Underline	U
Paste	V
Cut	X
Redo	Y
Undo	Z

PowerPoint for Beginners
POWERPOINT ESSENTIALS BOOK 1

M.L. HUMPHREY

CONTENTS

INTRODUCTION

The purpose of this guide is to introduce you to the basics of using Microsoft PowerPoint. If you've ever found yourself in a situation where you need to present to a larger audience than just a handful of people then you've probably needed PowerPoint. It's great for summarizing and organizing information and also the go-to software for creating presentation slides.

Of course, if you've ever been on the receiving end of a presentation made by a large consulting firm then you've probably seen how PowerPoint can be abused and misused to the point of ridiculousness. (Or is it just me that thinks that crowding a slide with so much information there's no way it could actually be legible if presented on a screen is wrong?)

Anyway. This guide will walk you through the basics of how to use PowerPoint. By the time you finish reading this guide you will be fully capable of creating a basic PowerPoint presentation that includes text, pictures, and/or tables of information. You will also be able to format any text you enter and will know how to add notes to your slides, animate your slides so that each bullet point appears separately, and launch your presentation as a slide show or print a copy or handouts.

(And, yes, this guide will even allow you to create overly-crowded dense slides with too much information on them if that's really what you want to do.)

As you can see, I will also be sprinkling in my opinion throughout this guide so it isn't just going to be how to do things in PowerPoint but why you might want to do it in a certain way.

There are other aspects to PowerPoint that I'm not going to cover in this guide. For example, we're not going to discuss how to use SmartArt.

The goal of this guide is to give you enough information on how to create a basic presentation without overwhelming you with information you may not need. I do, however, end with a discussion of your help options for learning more should you need it.

This guide is written using PowerPoint 2013. If you have a version of PowerPoint prior to 2007 your interface will look very different from mine. At this point, it's probably worth paying to upgrade to a more recent version of Office for anyone using a pre-2007 version, but that's up to you. If you do stick with an older version of PowerPoint, you'll be limited in terms of the resources you can find to help you when you get stuck. (Also the themes that will be discussed in this guide may not exist in your version.)

If you've already read *Word for Beginners* or *Excel for Beginners*, some portions of this guide will be familiar to you because the text options in PowerPoint work much the same way they do in Word and Excel. Also, the PowerPoint interface is structured in much the same way as both Word and Excel. If you're familiar with one of those programs already you should find PowerPoint easier to learn than someone who is new to all three.

Alright then. Now that you know what this guide is going to cover, let's get started with some basics.

BASIC TERMINOLOGY

Before we get started, I want to make sure that we're on the same page in terms of terminology. Some of this will be standard to anyone talking about these programs and some of it is my personal quirky way of saying things, so best to skim through if nothing else.

Tab

I refer to the menu choices at the top of the screen (File, Home, Insert, Design, Transitions, Animations, Slide Show, Review, and View) as tabs. If you click on one you'll see that the way it's highlighted sort of looks like an old-time filing system.

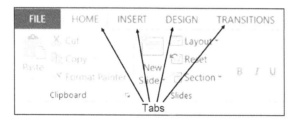

Each tab you select will show you different options. For example, in the image above, I have the Home tab selected and you can do various tasks such as cut/copy/paste, add new slides, change the slide layout, change fonts or font size or font color, change text formatting, add shapes, find/replace, etc. Other tabs give other options.

Click

If I tell you to click on something, that means to use your mouse (or trackpad) to move the arrow on the screen over to a specific location and left-click or right-click on the option. (See the next definition for the difference between left-click and right-click).

If you left-click, this selects the item. If you right-click, this generally creates a dropdown list of options to choose from. If I don't tell you which to do, left- or right-click, then left-click.

Left-click/Right-click

If you look at your mouse or your trackpad, you generally have two flat buttons to press. One is on the left side, one is on the right. If I say left-click that means to press down on the button on the left. If I say right-click that means press down on the button on the right.

Now, as I sadly learned when I had to upgrade computers, not all trackpads have the left- and right-hand buttons. In that case, you'll basically want to press on either the bottom left-hand side of the trackpad or the bottom right-hand side of the trackpad. Since you're working blind it may take a little trial and error to get the option you want working. (Or is that just me?)

Select or Highlight

If I tell you to select text, that means to left-click at the end of the text you want to select, hold that left-click, and move your cursor to the other end of the text you want to select.

Another option is to use the Shift key. Go to one end of the text you want to select. Hold down the shift key and use the arrow keys to move to the other end of the text you want to select. If you arrow up or down, that will select an entire row at a time.

With both methods, which side of the text you start on doesn't matter. You can start at the end and go to the beginning or start at the beginning and go to the end. Just start at one end or the other of the text you want to select.

The text you've selected will then be highlighted in gray.

If you need to select text that isn't touching you can do this by selecting your first section of text and then holding down the Ctrl key and selecting your second section of text using your mouse. (You can't arrow to the second section of text or you'll lose your already selected text.)

Dropdown Menu

If you right-click on a PowerPoint slide, you will see what I'm going to refer to as a dropdown menu. (Sometimes it will actually drop upward if you're towards the bottom of the document.)

A dropdown menu provides you a list of choices to select from like this one that you'll see if you right-click on a Title Slide in a presentation:

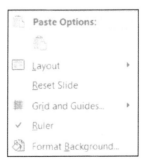

There are also dropdown menus available for some of the options listed under the tabs at the top of the screen. For example, if you go to the Home tab, you'll see small arrows below or next to some of the options, like the Layout option and the Section option in the Slides section. Clicking on those little arrows will give you a dropdown menu with a list of choices to choose from like this one for Layout:

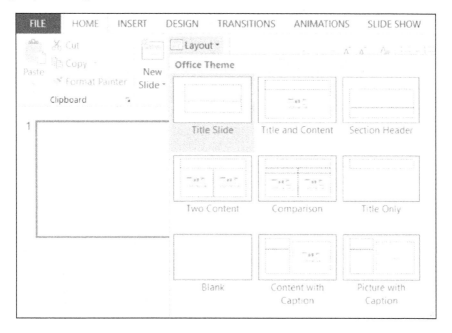

Expansion Arrows

I don't know the official word for these, but you'll also notice at the bottom right corner of most of the sections in each tab that there are little arrows. If you click on one of those arrows PowerPoint will bring up a more detailed set of options, usually through a dialogue box (which we'll discuss next).

In the Home tab, for example, there are expansion arrows for Clipboard, Font, Paragraph, and Drawing. Holding your mouse over the arrow will give a brief description of what clicking on the expansion arrow will do like here for the Clipboard section on the Home tab:

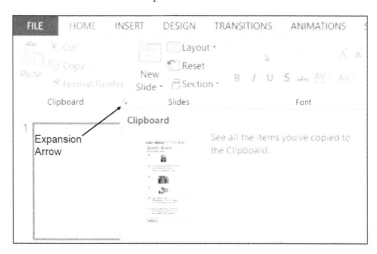

Dialogue Box

Dialogue boxes are pop-up boxes that cover specialized settings. As just mentioned, if you click on an expansion arrow, it will often open a dialogue box that contains more choices than are visible in that section. When you right-click on a PowerPoint content slide and choose Font, Paragraph, or Hyperlink that also opens dialogue boxes.

Dialogue boxes often allow the most granular level of control over an option. For example, this is the Font dialogue box which you can see has more options available than in the Font section of the Home tab.

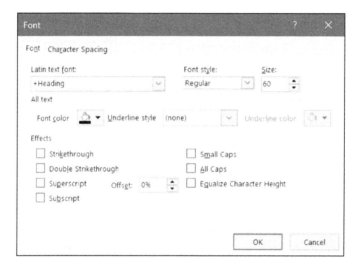

Scroll Bar

PowerPoint has multiple scroll bars that are normally visible. One is on the right-hand side of the slides that are displayed to the left of your screen (but only when there are enough slides to require scrolling). The other is on the right-hand side of the current slide that you're viewing in the main display section of PowerPoint when there are at least two slides in your presentation.

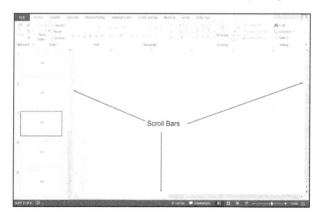

You can either click in the space above or below the scroll bar to move up or down a small amount or you can left-click on the bar, hold the left-click, and drag the bar up or down to move more quickly. You can also use the arrows at the top and the bottom to move up and down through your document.

In the default view where you can see an entire slide in the main screen, the right-hand scroll bar will move you through your presentation. Clicking on the scroll bar for the left-hand pane will keep you on the current slide but show you other slides in the presentation. (That you can then click on if you want to go to that slide.)

I generally use the scroll bar on the left-hand side when I use one at all.

You won't normally see a scroll bar at the bottom of the screen, but it is possible. This would happen if you ever change the zoom level to the point that you're not seeing the entire presentation slide on the screen. (To test this, click on the main slide, go to the View tab, click on Zoom, and choose 400%. You should now see a scroll bar on the bottom of the main section where your current slide is visible.)

Arrow

If I ever tell you to arrow to the left or right or up or down, that just means use your arrow keys. This will move your cursor to the left one space, to the right one space, up one line, or down one line. If you're at the end of a line and arrow to the right, it will take you to the beginning of the next line. If you're at the beginning of a line and arrow to the left, it will take you to the end of the last line.

Cursor

There are two possible meanings for cursor. One is the one I just used. When you're clicked into a PowerPoint slide, you will see that there is a blinking line. This indicates where you are in the document. If you type text, each letter will appear where the cursor was at the time you typed it. The cursor will move (at least in the U.S. and I'd assume most European versions) to the right as you type. This version of the cursor should be visible at all times unless you have text selected.

The other type of cursor is the one that's tied to the movement of your mouse or trackpad. When you're typing, it will not be visible. But stop typing and move your mouse or trackpad, and you'll see it. If the cursor is positioned over your text, it will look somewhat like a tall skinny capital I. If you move it up to the menu options or off to the sides, it becomes a white arrow. (Except for when you position it over any option under the tabs that can be typed in such as Font Size or Font where it will once again look like a skinny capital I.)

Usually I won't refer to your cursor, I'll just say, "click" or "select" or whatever action you need to take with it, and moving the cursor to that location will be implied.

Quick Access Toolbar

In the very top left corner of your screen when you have PowerPoint open you should see a series of symbols. These are part of the Quick Access Toolbar.

You can customize what options appear here by clicking on the downward pointing arrow with a line above it that you see at the very end of the list and then clicking on the commands you want to have available there. (If you don't want a command available, do the same thing. Click on the dropdown arrow and then click on the command so it's no longer selected.) Selected commands have a checkmark next to them.

The Quick Access Toolbar can be useful if there's something you're doing repeatedly that's located on a different tab than something else you're doing repeatedly. I, for example, have customized my toolbar in Word to allow me to easily insert section breaks without having to move away from the Home tab.

To see what command a symbol in your toolbar represents, hold your cursor over the symbol.

Control Shortcuts

Throughout this document, I'm going to mention various control shortcuts that you can use to perform tasks like save, copy, cut, and paste. Each of these will be written as Ctrl + a capital letter, but when you use the shortcut on your computer you don't need to use the capitalized version of the letter. For example, holding down the Ctrl key and the s key at the same time will save your document. I'll write this as Ctrl + S, but that just means hold down the key that says ctrl and the s key at the same time.

Undo

One of the most powerful control shortcuts in PowerPoint (or any program, really) is the Undo option. If you do something you didn't mean to or that you want to take back, use Ctrl + Z to undo it. This should step you back one step and reverse whatever you just did. If you need to reverse more than one step, just keep using Ctrl + Z until you've undone everything you wanted to undo.

(There is also a small left-pointing arrow in the Quick Access Toolbar that will do the same thing.)

ABSOLUTE BASICS

Now let's discuss some absolute basics, like opening, closing, saving, and deleting presentations.

Starting a New PowerPoint Presentation

To start a brand new PowerPoint presentation, I click on PowerPoint 2013 from my applications menu or the shortcut I have on my computer's taskbar. If you're already in PowerPoint and want to open a new PowerPoint presentation you can go to the File tab and choose New from the left-hand menu.

Any of these options will bring up a list of various presentation themes you can choose from. I usually use one of these when I'm doing a non-corporate presentation rather than try to create a presentation from scratch.

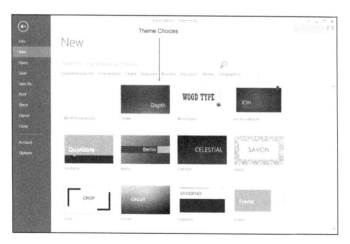

Clicking on any of the themes will bring up a secondary display where you can then use the "More Images" arrows at the bottom to see what the various slides in the presentation will look like. With most of these options you can also click on variant versions that are shown to the right side that are generally the same in terms of layout and font but provide different color options.

For example, the Vapor Trail theme has two options with a black background and two with a white background.

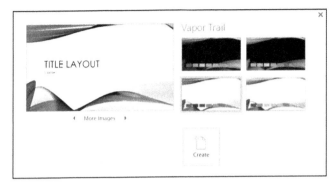

Once you find a template that you like click on Create and PowerPoint will open a new presentation for you that has the Title Slide for that template shown.

As you choose which theme you're going to use, I'd encourage you to think of your potential audience and which presentation is most appropriate for that audience. For example, I personally like the look of Vapor Trail but I would never use it for a presentation to one of my corporate clients. It's too artistic for that audience and the type of consulting I do.

If you have a company-provided template it's best to open that template (discussed next) and work from there.

You can also use Ctrl + N to start a new presentation but that will bring up a Title Slide that has no theme and is just plain white. (You can then choose a theme from the Design tab in PowerPoint as we'll discuss later.)

Opening an Existing PowerPoint File

To open an existing PowerPoint file you can go to the folder where the file is saved and double-click on the file name. Or you can open PowerPoint without selecting a file and it will provide a list of recent documents to choose from on the left-hand side of the screen.

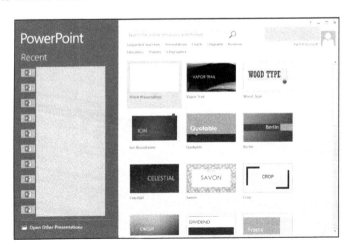

There is also an option at the bottom of that list of recent files to Open Other Presentations. If you click on that it will take you to the Open option that is normally available under the File tab. If you're already in PowerPoint you can access this option by going to the File tab and choosing Open from the left-hand menu or using Ctrl + O.

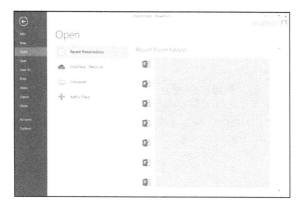

If the document you need is listed, left-click on it once and it will open. (As long as you haven't renamed the file or moved it since it was last opened. In that case, you'll need to navigate to where the file is saved and open it that way, either within PowerPoint or outside of PowerPoint.)

If the document you need is not listed in the list of Recent Presentations or has been moved or renamed since it was last used, click on Computer. (Or OneDrive if you store files in the cloud.) You can then navigate to the folder where the file you need is saved by either clicking on the folder name under Current Folder or Recent Folders (if listed) or by clicking on Browse to bring up the Open dialogue box.

Saving a PowerPoint File

To quickly save your presentation, you can use Ctrl + S or click on the small image of a floppy disk in the top left corner of the screen above File. For a document you've already saved that will overwrite the prior version of the document with the current version and will keep the file name, file type, and file location the same.

If you try to save a file that has never been saved before, it will automatically default to the Save As option which requires that you specify where to save the file, give it a name, and designate the file type. There are defaults for name and format, but you'll want to change the name of the document to something better than Document2.

You can also choose Save As when you want to change the location of a file, the name of a file, or the file type. (With respect to file type, I sometimes need to, for example, save a presentation file as a .pdf file or a .jpg file instead.) To do so, go to File and choose Save As from there.

The first choice you have to make for Save As is where you want to save the file. I see a list of my most recent seven folders listed and can also choose to Browse if I want to use a different location than one of the folders listed.

When you click on the location where you want to save the file, this will bring up the Save As dialogue box. Type in the name you want for the file and choose the file type. My file type defaults to PowerPoint Presentation (.pptx), but that can be changed using the dropdown next to "Save as type."

If you had already saved the file and you choose to Save As but keep the same location, name, and format as before, PowerPoint will overwrite the previous version of the file just like it would have if you'd used Save.

If you just want to rename a file, it's actually best to close the file and then go to where the file is saved and rename it that way rather than use Save As. Using Save As will keep the original of the file as well as creating the newer version. That's great when you want version control (which is rarely needed for PowerPoint), but not when you just wanted to rename your file from Great Presentation v22 to Great Presentation FINAL.

Renaming a PowerPoint File

As discussed above, you can use Save As to give an existing file a new name, but that approach will leave you with two versions of the file, one with the old name and one with the new name. If you just want to change the name of the existing file, close it and then navigate to where you've saved it. Click on the file name once to select it, click on it a second time to highlight the name, and then type in the new name you want to use, replacing the old one. If you rename the file this way outside of PowerPoint, there will only be one version of the file left, the one with the new name you wanted.

Just be aware that if you rename a file by navigating to where it's located and changing the name you won't be able to access the file from the Recent Presentations list under Open since that will still list the old name which no longer exists.

Deleting a PowerPoint File

You can't delete a PowerPoint file from within PowerPoint. You need to close the file you want to delete and then navigate to where the file is stored and delete the file there without opening it. Once you've located the file, click on the file name. (Only enough to select it. Make sure you haven't double-clicked and highlighted the name which will delete the file name but not the file.) Next, choose Delete from the menu at the top of the screen, or right-click and choose Delete from the dropdown menu.

Closing a PowerPoint File

To close a PowerPoint file click on the X in the top right corner or go to File and then choose Close. (You can also use Ctrl + W, but I never have.)

If no changes have been made to the document since you saved it last, it will just close.

If changes have been made, PowerPoint should ask you if you want to save those changes. You can either choose to save them, not save them, or cancel closing the document and leave it open. I almost always default to saving any changes. If I'm in doubt about whether I'd be overwriting something important, I cancel and choose to Save As and save the current file as a later version of the document just in case (e.g., Great Presentation v2).

If you had copied an image or a large block of text, you may also have a box pop up asking if you want to keep that image or text when you close the document. Usually the answer to this is no, but if you had planned on pasting that image or text somewhere else and hadn't yet done so, you can say to keep it on the clipboard.

YOUR WORKSPACE

Whether you choose to start a brand new file or open an existing file, you'll end up in the main workspace for PowerPoint. It looks something like this:

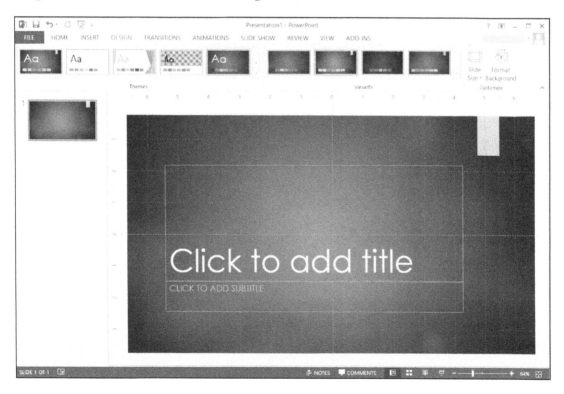

We'll walk through this in more detail in the *Working with Your Presentation Slides* section but I just wanted you to see right now that there's a left-hand pane that shows all of the slides in the presentation and then a main section of the screen that shows the slide you're currently working on.

For a new presentation there's just the one slide.

* * *

For a fully-built presentation, it will look more like this:

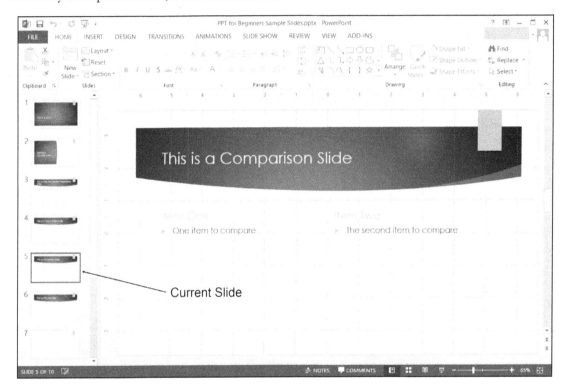

The slide you're currently seeing in the main section of the screen will have a dark border around it in the left-hand pane and your slides will be numbered starting at 1.

Across the top are your menu tabs and there are scroll bars for both the left-hand pane and the main section as well. Along the bottom are a couple of additional pieces of information or settings, including a zoom option in the bottom right corner.

CHOOSING A
PRESENTATION THEME

If you use Ctrl + N to start a new presentation you will have a blank presentation with no design elements. As a beginner, I would suggest that you use one of the PowerPoint designs for your presentation rather than create a design from scratch. (And the rest of this guide assumes that's the choice you're going to make. I do not cover in this guide how to build a presentation from scratch. That's intermediate-level.)

Also, sometimes you're going to choose a theme when you start a new presentation and then decide that that design doesn't work for your purposes and want to change it.

It's very easy to switch between design themes in PowerPoint, so let's walk through how to do it.

Open the presentation you want to change.

Go to the Design tab.

You should see that the Themes section takes up most of the screen.

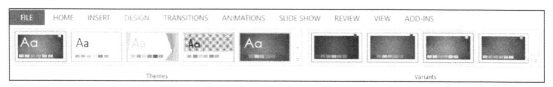

The far left-hand thumbnail in that section is your current design template.

On the right-hand side of the Design tab you'll see a separate section titled Variants.

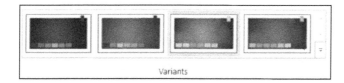

Variants

This will show different color variations on your current theme. So with the Ion theme if I wanted a purple background instead of a blue one, I could click on that image in the Variant section to change my presentation.

The rest of the thumbnails in the Themes section are other design templates you can choose from.

I would recommend having a Title and Content Slide visible in your presentation and using that to decide. (Right-click in the left-hand pane and choose New Slide to add one.) The reason for this is that some of the design templates put the header section of the slide at the bottom instead of the top. Or they have a colored background on all of the slides instead of just the Title Slide. You'll want to know that before you choose that theme since it can significantly impact the effectiveness of your presentation.

(My recommendation would be to choose a theme with a white background for the main slides and with the title section at the top. At least for standard corporate presentations.)

To see what your slides will look like before you change the theme, just hold your cursor over each thumbnail image in the Theme section of the Design tab and the slide in the main screen will change to show that theme.

To select that theme, click on the thumbnail image. All of your slides should then change over to the new theme and that thumbnail should now be visible as the left-most thumbnail in the Theme section.

(If you are using sections in your presentation, something we won't cover in this guide, then only the slides in your current section will change to the new theme. So using sections would be a way to use multiple themes in a single presentation, although I wouldn't recommend doing that. The point of using a design theme is that it provides cohesiveness to a presentation.)

POWERPOINT SLIDE TYPES

There are a number of slide types available to you in PowerPoint. Probably more than you'll actually need. But I wanted to run through them real quick before we go any further because I'm going to occasionally refer to a slide type and I want you to know what I'm talking about when I do so.

The images below use the Ion Boardroom theme. If you want to change the slide type of a slide, you can right-click on that slide, go to Layout, and choose from the listed options there. Not all themes or templates will have all slide types in them. And different themes may have the elements in different locations on the slide. For example, some put the header at the bottom instead of the top.

You can put together a perfectly adequate presentation with just the Title Slide, Section Header, and Title and Content slide types, but I'll walk through most of the others for you just in case.

Title Slide

The Title slide is the default first slide for a presentation. It has a section for adding a title and a subtitle and, if you choose one of the templates provided in PowerPoint, a background that covers the rest of the slide and matches your chosen theme.

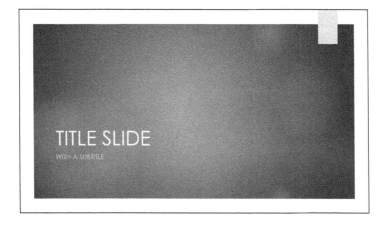

Section Header

If you are going to have sections within your presentation, then you'll want to separate them using a Section Header slide. Like the title slides above this slide will have a colored background that matches your theme. It will generally have the text in a different position or using a different font or font size to distinguish it from the title slide or will use a different color for the background or move the background image to a new location.

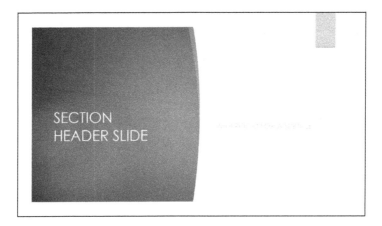

Title and Content Slide

The Title and Content slide is the one I use for most of my presentations. It has a section where you can describe what the slide is discussing and then a content box where you can add text, images, etc. When you're doing a basic presentation with a bulleted set of talking points, this is the slide that you'll probably use the most often.

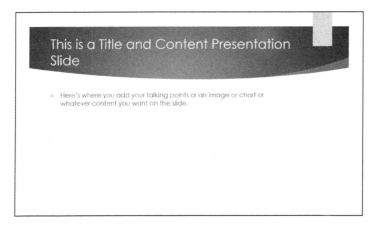

While most themes will have the title portion at the top (and I think that's the best choice for a corporate presentation) some of the themes have the title portion at the bottom or off to the side, so check your theme before you choose it. For example, this is the Title and Content Slide from the Slice theme using the exact same text as the image above.

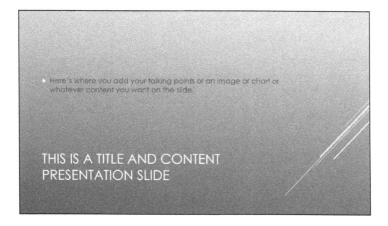

As you can also see above, content slides will sometimes have a colored background and sometimes will not depending on the theme you choose. Also, some themes use all caps in the title section and some do not. If you're switching between themes, be careful with this because it's easy with a theme that uses all caps to not pay attention to your capitalization and then move to a theme that uses upper and lower case and have some words capitalized and some not.

Two Content

The Two Content slide is another content slide. This slide has a section for a title and then two content boxes. It can be a good choice for when you want to either have two separate bulleted lists side by side or when you want to have text next to an image. You put the text in one of the boxes and the image in the other.

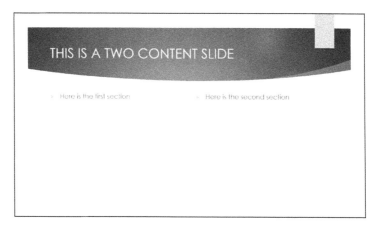

Comparison

The Comparison slide is also a content slide. It's much like the Two Content slide except it has added sections directly above each of the two text boxes where you can put header text to describe the contents of each of the boxes below.

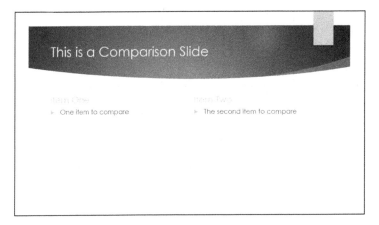

Title Only

The Title Only slide is a content slide that just has the title section and nothing else below it. You can add elements to the body of this slide, such as a text box or an image, but there is no pre-defined space for it like with the prior content slide types. It will have the same background as content slides for your selected theme.

Content With Caption

The Content With Caption slide is another content slide. In this one the title section covers half of the screen and there are two text boxes where you can add text, images, etc. One is below the title and the other takes up the other side of the slide.

Picture With Caption

The Picture With Caption slide is a slide you'd probably use for an appendix or some information you're calling out separate from the main presentation. It has a large section for a picture and then a section for title and text. (In the picture below I added a stock photo of some keyboard keys to the section for the photo and it took a portion of the image and scaled it to fit.)

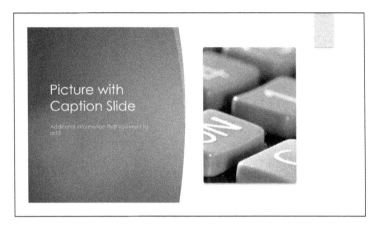

Quote With Caption

The Quote With Caption slide is a slide that has quote marks around the main text section and then a smaller text box for an attribution of who said the quote as well as a larger text box for comments.

Blank

The blank slide has the same background as the other content slides for your chosen theme, but nothing else.

Other

Some themes will have even more pre-formatted slide types you can use. The Ion Boardroom theme has a three-column version as well as a few others I didn't cover here. And some won't have this many. If you need a specific slide type, be sure to check that that slide type is available before you get too far into working with your chosen theme.

WORKING WITH YOUR PRESENTATION SLIDES

In this chapter we're going to assume that you've created a brand new presentation using one of the templates. So now you find yourself in PowerPoint with a title slide visible on the left-hand side and in the main screen:

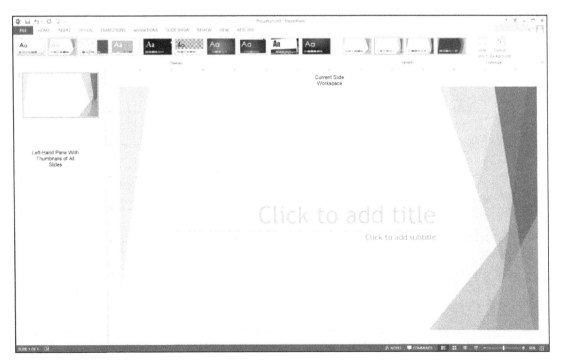

First things first, let's talk about what you're seeing. On the left-hand side of the screen are thumbnail (i.e., small) images of your slides. As you add new slides to your presentation they'll appear in this left-hand pane. In the center of the screen and taking up most of the space is the current slide you are working on. Because there's only this one slide to begin with it's going to be your title slide when you first open the file.

You can click on any of the slides in the left-hand pane or you can click on the slide in the center. Depending on which one you're clicked into, you'll be able to do different things such as add text to a slide or move a slide to a different location.

Let's start with the left-hand pane because that's where you'll work to change the positioning of your slides as well as add new ones or delete ones you no longer want.

If you right-click into the blank space below the title slide, you'll see that you have the option to add a new slide or add a new section. (In the hundreds of presentations I've done I've never needed to use sections so we're going to set that aside as an intermediate topic.) If you had copied slides from another presentation or even this one, you could also paste them as well, but since we haven't copied any slides yet that's not actually an available option. So all you have is the New Slide option.

If you choose that option, PowerPoint will insert a Title and Content slide for you. (Since this is the most common slide type I use for inputting information, it's convenient that PowerPoint defaults to that slide type.)

Now that we have two slides, let's discuss how you can select a slide or slides and how to move slides within your presentation.

Selecting a Slide or Slides

To select a single slide, you simply left-click on the slide where it's visible in the left-hand pane. When a slide is selected it should have a darker border around it. In my version of PowerPoint that border is red.

If you want to select more than once slide, you can select the first slide and then hold down the Ctrl key as you left-click on the next slide or slides that you want to select. When you do this each slide you click on will have that dark border around it.

Slides do not need to be next to one another for you to select them this way.

If you have a range of slides that you want to select, you can use the Shift key instead. Click on the slide at the top or the bottom of the range of slides you want, hold down the Shift key, and then click on the slide at the other end of the range of slides you want. All slides within that range, including the first slide you clicked and the second slide you clicked, should now have a dark border around them.

So, for example, if I want to select the first four slides in my presentation, I can click on the first slide, hold down the Shift key, and then click on the fourth slide. Or I could click on the fourth slide, hold down the Shift key, and then click on the first slide. As long as the slides you click on are at the beginning and end of your range of desired slides, you will select all of them.

(You can also combine methods of selecting slides to, for example, select a range of slides using Shift and then select an additional slide using the Ctrl key.)

No matter how many slides you select, the main screen will only show one of them.

To remove your selection of multiple slides, click in the gray area around any of the slides or on the main presentation slide.

Moving a Slide or Slides

The easiest way to move a slide or slides to a different position within your presentation is to select the slide(s) (as noted above) and then left-click and drag the slide(s) to the new location. As you move your chosen slide(s) you'll see the slides in the left-hand pane moving upward or downward to leave a space for your slides to be inserted. (It sounds weird, but just try it and you'll see what I'm talking about.)

If you've selected more than one slide, you can left-click on any of the slides you've selected and drag and all of the slides will move to the new location even if they weren't next to one another before.

Cutting a Slide or Slides

If you right-click on a slide or slides that you've selected and choose Cut from the dropdown menu, you can remove the slide or slides from their current location in the presentation. You can also do this by selecting the slide(s) and then using Ctrl + X.

Where cutting differs from deleting, which will have the same effect of removing the slides, is that cutting the slides allows you to move them elsewhere. You could cut them and then paste them into another location in that same presentation (using Paste which we'll discuss in a moment) or you could paste them into another PowerPoint presentation.

Cutting only deletes slides if you cut them and then choose not to put them in a new location.

Usually you can just select and drag slides into a new location within your presentation as we just discussed above, but if you have a very long presentation (say 200 slides) and want to move a slide from the beginning to the end, for example, it can be faster to cut the slide, scroll down to the end, and then paste.

You can also cut a slide by clicking on it, going to the Clipboard section of the Home tab, and choosing Cut from there.

Copying a Slide or Slides

If you right-click on a slide or slides that you've selected and choose Copy from the dropdown men, you can keep a version of the slides exactly where they were while creating a copy of those slides that you can then move into a new presentation or move to a new location within your existing presentation. (Using Paste which we'll discuss next.)

You can also use Ctrl + C to copy a set of slides. So select the slides you want to copy and then type Ctrl + C.

Where copy differs from cut is that it leaves the original version of the slides where they were. You now end up with two identical copies of that set of slides and you can place that second copy of the slides wherever you need them, either in your current presentation or another one.

(I tend to use Duplicate Slide instead when I'm working in a presentation. We'll talk about that one in a moment.)

You can also copy a slide by clicking on it, going to the Clipboard section of the Home tab, and choosing Copy from there.

Pasting a Slide or Slides

If you copy or cut a slide or slides and want to use them elsewhere, you need to paste them into that new location. You can do a basic paste by clicking into the space where you want to put those slides (so between two existing slides or in the gray space at the end of the presentation, for example) and using Ctrl + V.

If you are clicked onto a slide when you paste, your copied or cut slides will be pasted in below that slide.

You can also right-click where you want to paste a slide and choose from the paste options.

The first option, which has a small a in the bottom right corner, is Use Destination Theme. If you're cutting or copying and pasting within an existing presentation this won't mean much. But I've used this one often when working with a corporate PowerPoint template where someone drafted a presentation without using the corporate template and then handed it off to me and asked me to make it look like it should. (Always a pleasure when that happens.)

In those cases, I copy all of the slides from the version of the presentation I've been given and paste it into the corporate template using the destination theme option. This will convert the slides you pasted in from whatever theme they were using to your corporate template theme.

(You can test this for yourself by cutting a slide from your current presentation, changing the theme of your current presentation, and then right-clicking and pasting the slide back into your presentation using the Use Destination Theme option.)

Use Destination Theme is also what happens when you just use Ctrl + V.

The second paste option you have, the one with the paintbrush in the bottom right corner, is Keep Source Formatting. This does what it says, it keeps the formatting the slide(s) already had. Sometimes it's important to do this especially if you've done a lot of custom work on a slide and don't want your images, charts, etc. resized when you move them into a new presentation.

The third paste option, the one with a photo icon in the bottom right corner, is to paste a slide in as a Picture. That means the slide can no longer be edited. It's like someone took a snapshot of that slide and now you just have that snapshot. If you try to use this option with multiple slides only the first slide will paste in.

I would expect you won't use this one often.

You can also paste slides by going to the Clipboard section of the Home tab and choosing Paste from there. The more advanced options are available by clicking on the arrow under Paste.

Adding a New Slide

If you right-click on an existing slide in the presentation or in the gray area in the left-hand pane, you can add a new slide by choosing New Slide from the dropdown menu.

If you click on a slide and then choose New Slide, the slide that is added to your presentation will match the type of the slide you were clicked onto when you made that choice.

If you click in the gray area to add a slide, the slide type will match the slide directly above where you had clicked. (With the exception of a Title slide. In that case the new slide added will be a Title and Content slide.)

You can also go to the Slides section of the Home tab and click on New Slide there. If you use the dropdown arrow next to New Slide you can choose the layout for the new slide before you add it.

Duplicating a Slide

If you want to create a duplicate of an existing slide (something I do when I've created custom formatting and don't want to have to recreate it on each slide), you can right-click on a slide and choose Duplicate Slide. This will create an exact duplicate of the slide you right-clicked on.

You can also duplicate a slide by clicking on the slide, going to the Clipboard section of the Home tab, clicking on the arrow next to Copy, and choosing Duplicate from the dropdown menu.

Deleting a Slide

To delete a slide, you can click on that slide and then hit the Delete or Backspace key. Either one will work. Or you can right-click on that slide and choose Delete Slide from the dropdown menu.

Choosing the Slide Layout

To change the type of slide, select the slide or slides you need to change, right-click, go to Layout, and select the type you want from the available options. Each one will have the type listed as well as a small thumbnail image.

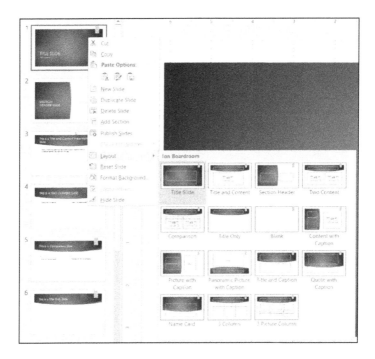

Different themes will have different options available. For example, the Ion theme has a Quote with Caption slide option that is not available in the Integral theme.

If you're using a custom theme (such as a corporate one) and don't have example slides in the presentation of the type you need, you may not have that layout option available to choose even though it exists in your corporate template. (This is why if I'm ever working with a corporate template I leave the sample slides in my presentation until I'm done and then delete them at the very last minute to make sure I won't need one of those choices.)

PowerPoint will do its best to change your current slide over to the chosen layout, but if you already had content in a slide when you changed the layout be sure to review each slide to make sure the way that PowerPoint changed the slide to the new layout makes sense.

You can also select a slide or slides, go to the Slides section of the Home tab, click on the dropdown arrow next to Layout, and choose your layout from there.

Resetting a Slide

If you makes changes to the layout of a slide, by for example changing the size of the text boxes or their location, and want to go back to the original layout for that slide type, you can right-click on the slide and choose Reset Slide from the dropdown menu. According to PowerPoint, this will "reset the position, size, and formatting of the slide placeholders to their default settings."

You can also click on a slide and go to the Slides section of the Home tab and choose Reset from there.

ADDING TEXT TO A PRESENTATION SLIDE

Now let's turn our attention from the left-hand pane to the main section of your PowerPoint screen where your current slide is shown.

Adding text to an existing slide is very simple. You click and type.

For example, here, is a Title slide:

You can see that the slide says "CLICK TO ADD TITLE" and "CLICK TO ADD SUBTITLE". And it's almost that easy. Click on where it say that and type. Click away when you're done. You will now be able to see whatever text you typed in that space and formatted according to that theme. (Usually that will cover text color and whether the text appears in all caps or not.)

If you add a different type of slide, such as a Title and Content slide, you'll see that that slide also has sections for adding text. It says "CLICK TO ADD TITLE" and "CLICK TO ADD TEXT". Many of the themes are pre-formatted to create bulleted lists that match the theme. As soon as you type, your text will be shown as part of a bulleted list. And each time you hit Enter a new bullet point will appear.

If you need to create subpoints, use the tab key to indent the line before you start typing your text. In some templates this will also change the type of bullet used or change the size of the bullet.

If you need to remove an indent, use Shift+Tab before your start typing.

■ **And another one.**
 – *Tab before typing to indent, note the different bullet point style*
 – *And then just hit Enter*
■ **Shift + Tab before typing to remove the indent**

For lines that have already been added where you need to adjust the indent, click to the left of the first letter in that line and then use Tab or Shift + Tab to adjust the indent. You can also use the Decrease List Level and Increase List Level options in the Paragraph section of the Home tab. They're the ones with lines with an arrow pointing either left or right in the middle of the top row.

By default the PowerPoint themes use fonts and font sizes that are legible for a presentation given on a projector. But the slides are also dynamic in the sense that as you add more and more and more to a slide the text in that slide will adjust in size to fit in the text box on the slide. Be careful with this.

For two reasons. First, if you let the font size get too small, no one will be able to read your slide. Why put together a presentation that no one can read?

Second, because this can happen on a slide-by-slide basis it can create a disjointed presentation. If one slide has bullet points in a 20 point size and another has bullet points in a 14 point size and another has them in an 11 point size, even if the font and colors are consistent across slides it can be jarring.

I try when I can to make the font size consistent across slides. So if I do have a very busy slide that requires a smaller font size than the default, then I'll usually change all other slides in the presentation to match that font size. (Easier to simplify the language instead, but that's not always an option when working on group projects.)

Be especially careful about legibility with respect to your subpoints. Each level of subpoint generally uses a smaller font size than the last. It's easy to get to the point where the last level can't be read. I'd advise limiting your bulleted lists to three levels at most and ideally just two levels to avoid this issue.

(A good template will limit this. So, for example, the Ion Boardroom theme stops decreasing font size when the font size reaches 12 point.)

* * *

If you need to cut, copy, or paste text from within a slide, it works much the same way as it did for the slides in the left-hand pane.

To cut text, highlight the text you want to cut and then use Ctrl + X or go to the Clipboard section of the Home tab and choose Cut from there. You can also right-click and choose Cut from the dropdown menu.

As you'll recall, cutting text removes it from its current location but still allows you to paste that text elsewhere.

To copy text, highlight the text you want to copy and then use Ctrl + C or to go to the Clipboard section of the Home tab and choose Copy from there. You can also right-click and choose Copy from the dropdown menu.

Copying keeps the text in its current location but also allows you to paste that text elsewhere.

To paste text, click on the location where you want to place the text you copied or cut and then use Ctrl + V. If you paste text this way it will take on the formatting of the location where you paste it. Your other options are to click where you want to paste the text and then go to the Clipboard section of the Home tab and click on the arrow under Paste or right-click.

This will give you the Paste Options list of choices:

The option with the lower case a in the bottom right corner will use the formatting of the location where you are pasting your text.

The option with the paintbrush in the bottom right corner will keep the formatting the text already had.

The option with the small picture in the bottom right corner will paste the selected text in as an image. (You will not be able to edit this text after it's pasted because it will no longer be considered text.)

The option with the large A in the bottom right corner, will paste as text only. (This should generally have the same result as pasting with the destination theme, the first option.)

(There are more specialized paste options available under the Clipboard option, but for a beginner level I don't think they're worth discussing here. If you want to look at them click on Paste Special from the dropdown.)

* * *

If you need to remove text you can either cut that text or you can use the Delete or Backspace keys. Backspace will delete text to the left of the cursor. Delete will delete text to the right of the cursor.

If you've highlighted the text you want to delete then either one will work.

Delete and Backspace can also delete bullet points or the numbers or letters in a numbered list.

FORMATTING TEXT IN A PRESENTATION

All of the templates include text that's of a pre-defined size and using a pre-selected font. If you can stick to the defaults, your life will be much easier because then you can simply add a new slide and everything will be all set to work together.

But it's quite possible that at some point in time you'll want to customize a font size or change the font used or maybe even the color of the font. So in this section we'll walk through how to do that. Just know that doing so will add complications to your life.

As soon as you type text into a presentation slide you should see that the Font section of the Home tab is not only visible but populated with values. (Before you add text it will be visible but grayed out.)

Let's walk through what you can do using these options. For each option, you need to have selected the text you want to edit before you make your choice.

Font

The top left option in the Font section is where you select the font for your presentation. The current font will be visible in the dropdown box.

If you want to change that font you can click on the dropdown arrow and choose from the list of available fonts. The list will show the theme fonts first, your recently used fonts next, and then all available fonts in alphabetical order.

If you start typing a font name that will take you to that portion of the alphabetical listing. So typing T in the white space shows Tahoma and takes me to the T section of the font listing.

For a font that's later in the alphabet, it's often easier to start typing the name, but there is a scroll bar on the right-hand side of the listing that you can use to move through your selections.

The name of the fonts are written in that font to give you an idea of what each font will look like when used.

Another option is to right-click on your text to bring up what I call the mini-formatting bar. It has a font dropdown menu just like the one on the Home tab that you can use to change the font.

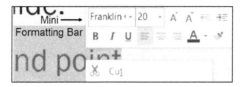

Or you can right-click on your text, choose Font from the dropdown menu, and then change the Latin Text Font box in the Font dialogue box to the font you want using the dropdown to select your font and then clicking on OK.

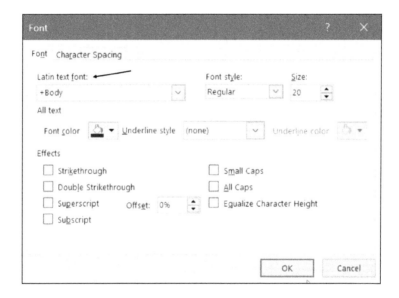

Font Size

The next option in the Font section of the Home tab is your font size. This determines how big the text is on the slide. 36 point is a good visible size for headers. 24 or 18 point is a good size for your main body text but you could probably go as small as 12 point. If you're doing handouts instead of a presentation, you can use 8 or 10 point for footnotes. Don't go smaller than that.

You have a number of options for changing your font size.

The first is to click into the box with the current font size and type a new value.

You can also click on the dropdown arrow next to the current font size and choose from one of the values in the dropdown.

Or you can use the Increase Font Size and Decrease Font Size options that are next to the font size dropdown menu and look like the letter A with either an up or a down arrow in the top right corner. If you use the increase and decrease font size options, the only values available to you are the ones in the dropdown menu.

You can also right-click and use the mini-formatting toolbar or right-click and choose Font from the dropdown menu and then change the font size in the Font dialogue box.

There are also control shortcuts for changing the font size upward or downward one level, but I honestly don't recommend learning them because I don't think you'll need them often enough to make it worthwhile. They are Ctrl + Shift + > to increase one font size and Ctrl + Shift + < to decrease one font size.

Font Color

The option in the bottom right corner of the Font section that looks like an A with a red line under it (at least when you first open PowerPoint—the line color can change as you work in PowerPoint) is where you can change the color of your text.

Click on the dropdown arrow and you'll see seventy different colors you can choose from.

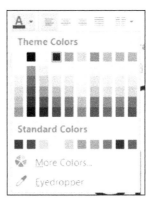

If you need a different or a custom color, click on More Colors. This will bring up the Colors dialogue box. On the Standard tab you can choose from the honeycomb of colors available by clicking on any of the colored squares. On the Custom tab you can input your own RGB values or HSL values. You can also click into the rainbow of colors above that or move the slider for different shades of a color. The color you've selected will show under New in the bottom right corner of the Colors dialogue box.

Another option available to you in PowerPoint is the eyedropper. When you click on the dropdown arrow for Font Color the bottom option in that list is the Eyedropper Text Fill. If you click on this and then click on a color in one of your presentation slides, PowerPoint will grab that color you clicked on. It will then be shown as a color you can use under Recent Colors in the color dropdown menu.

(I use the eyedropper often to pull a color from one of my book covers when I'm creating a related presentation. I import the cover, pull the color from it using the eyedropper, and then delete the cover.)

All of these color options are also available by right-clicking to pull up the mini-formatting bar.

You can also right-click, go to Font in the dropdown menu, and then on the Font tab of the Font dialogue box choose a font color from there. (The Font dialogue box dropdown does not, however, include the eyedropper option.)

Bolding Text

To bold text, highlight your text and click on the capital B on the left-hand side of the second row in the Font section of the Home tab.

You can also right-click on your selected text and click on the capital B in the mini-formatting bar.

Or you can use Ctrl + B after you've selected your text.

Or can right-click, choose Font from the dropdown menu, and then change the Font Style in the Font dialogue box to Bold. Or Bold Italic if you want both bold and italic.

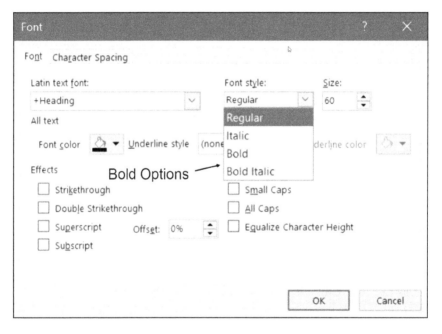

To remove bolding from text, select the text and either click on the capital B or use Ctrl + B once more. If you select text that is partially bolded and partially not bolded, you will need to do this twice because the first time will apply bolding to the entire selection and the second time will remove it from the entire selection.

You can also select your text, right-click, choose Font from the dropdown menu, and then change the Font Style to Regular.

Italicizing Text

To italicize text, select your text and click on the slanted I on the left-hand side of the second row in the Font section.

You can also click on the slanted I in the mini-formatting bar.

Or you can use Ctrl + I.

Or you can right-click, choose Font from the dropdown menu, and then change the Font Style in the Font dialogue box to Italic. (Or Bold Italic if you want both bold and italic.)

To remove italics from text, select the text and either click on the slanted I or use Ctrl + I once more. If you select text that is partially italicized and partially not, you will need to do this twice because the first time will apply italics to the entire selection and the second time will remove it from the entire selection.

You can also just right-click, choose Font from the dropdown menu, and then change the Font Style in the Font dialogue box to Regular.

Underlining Text

To underline text, click on the capital U with a line under it on the left-hand side of the second row in the Font section.

You can also click on the capital U with a line under it in the mini-formatting bar.

Or you can use Ctrl + U.

Or you can right-click, select Font from the dropdown menu, go to the Font dialogue box and choose from the dropdown menu next to Underline Style.

To remove underlining from text, select the text and either click on the capital U with a line under it or use Ctrl + U once more. If you select text that is partially underlined and partially not, you will need to do this twice because the first time will apply underlining to the entire selection and the second time will remove it from the entire selection.

You can also go to the Font dialogue box and change the Underline Style to (none).

If you want a different underline style than just the basic single line underline, it's best to use the Font dialogue box. (So right-click and choose Font from the dropdown menu and then change the Underline Style.) There you'll have the choice of a double-line or a bolder line than standard as well as dotted lines and wavy lines in various styles. (Don't get carried away here. Remember, clean and simple is better than fancy and complicated when trying to convey information to other people.)

To remove a non-standard underline, select the text and use Ctrl + U or click on the U in the Font section until there is no underline remaining. It will usually take two tries, because the first time will convert it to a standard underline. You can also just go back to the Font dialogue box and change the underline style back to none.

Change Case

If you want your text to be in all caps or if you have text that is already in all caps that you want to have in normal case, then you will need to change the case of that text.

You can do this in the Font section of the Home tab by clicking on the arrow next to the Aa in the bottom row on the right-hand side. This will give you a dropdown menu with choices for sentence case, lower case, upper case, capitalize each word, and toggle case.

Sentence case will capitalize the first letter of the first word in each sentence or text string.

Lower case will put all of the letters in lower case.

Upper case will put all of the letters in upper case.

Capitalize each word will capitalize the first letter of each word.

Toggle case will put the first letter of each word in lower case and all other letters in upper case.

Clear Text Formatting

If you've edited a text selection and want to return it to the default for that theme, you can select the text and then click on the small A with an eraser in the top right corner of the Font section. (If you hold your mouse over it, it will show as Clear All Formatting.)

This will change the selection to whatever font, font size, and font formatting would be appropriate for that location within that theme. It does not change the case of the letters but it will revert the font, font color, font size, and any bold, italics or underline back to the default for the theme.

Other

You'll note that there were a few other options available in the Font section of the Home tab (text shadowing, strikethrough, and character spacing) as well as additional options in the Font dialogue box.

I've chosen not to cover them here because I want to keep this guide focused on a basic level of PowerPoint presentation and those are ones I expect you wouldn't use often, but if there's a text effect you want to apply in a PowerPoint slide that I didn't cover, the Font section of the Home tab or right-clicking and choosing Font to bring up the Font dialogue box are a good place to start.

For more advanced text formatting you'll want to look to the Format tab under Drawing Tools that will appear when you click on any text in your presentation. That's intermediate level so we're not going to cover it here.

Next let's talk about paragraph-level formatting.

FORMATTING PARAGRAPHS IN A PRESENTATION

What we just talked about are formatting changes that you can make at the word level. But there are other changes you can make at the paragraph level. These are generally covered in the Paragraph section of the Home tab but some of them are also available in the mini formatting bar or by right-clicking and choosing Paragraph from the dropdown menu.

With the paragraph formatting options you don't have to highlight all of the text, you just need to be clicked onto the line or into the section you want to change. Let's start with one we already covered earlier, Decrease List Level and Increase List Level.

Decrease List Level/Increase List Level

A lot of PowerPoint presentations rely on using bulleted lists. And when you use a bulleted list you will often want to either indent the next line or decrease the indent of the next line.

To indent the next line, you can either click at the beginning of the line and use the Tab key. Or you can click anywhere on the line and use the Increase List Level option in the Paragraph section of the Home tab.

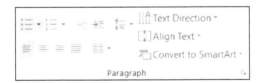

This is the one with a right-pointing arrow embedded in a series of lines that is on the top row and towards the middle on the left-hand side.

To decrease the indent on the next line, you can either click at the beginning of the line and use Shift + Tab (so hold down the Shift key and then the Tab key) or you can click anywhere on the line and use the Decease List Level option in the Paragraph section of the Home tab. This is the one with a left-pointing arrow embedded in a series of lines that is on the top row and also towards the middle on the left-hand side.

If the decrease list level option is grayed out (like it is in the picture above) that's because you're already at the far left-hand side and can't decrease the indent any further.

These options may or may not be available with plain text that isn't already bulleted or numbered. It will depend on where the text is located within the presentation slide.

Left-Align/Center/Right-Align a Paragraph

Your next option is to change the alignment of the text in your paragraph.

You have four options. You can have left-aligned text, meaning that each new line starts along the left-hand side of the text box. You can have centered text, meaning each line is centered within the text box. You can have right-aligned text, meaning each line ends along the right-hand side of the text box. Or you can have justified text meaning your text will be spread out across the text box so that it's even on both the right-hand edge and the left-hand edge.

All of this occurs within a single text box. If you look closely at the slide formats you'll see that each section with a "Click to add text" or similar message is within a box with a dotted line border. This is a text box. So any changes you make to your text to align it will be made not with respect to the entire PowerPoint slide but instead with respect to the boundaries of that specific text box.

Here are examples of all four options using a text box that has the same dimensions.

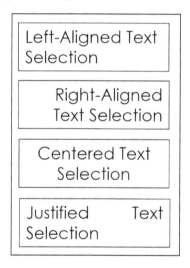

Depending on where your text is and what type it is, your selection will either apply to just the line of text you're clicked onto or all of the contents of the text box. So you may have to do some fiddling around to get the text aligned the way you want it. If you highlight rows of text and then make your alignment choice, all of the rows will change at once.

You can also right-click, choose Paragraph from the dropdown menu, and then choose your alignment option from Alignment dropdown menu in the General section of the Paragraph dialogue box. That also gives you the option to have distributed text.

Top/Middle/Bottom Align Text

You can also align text within a text box along the top, middle, or bottom of that text box. To choose which alignment option you want, go to the Paragraph section of the Home tab and click on the arrow next to Align Text in the middle on the right-hand side of the section.

Choose the option you want from the dropdown menu. Top-aligned text will have the first row at the top of the text box. Bottom-aligned text will have the last row at the bottom of the text box. Middle-aligned text will have the rows of text centered between the top and bottom of the text box

Your choice will apply to all text within the text box.

Using Multiple Columns

If you want your text displayed on a slide in multiple columns you have two choices. First, you can choose a slide layout that has two equally sized sections like the Two Content slide format and then input your text into both of those boxes, split evenly across the two boxes.

Or you can use the multiple column formatting option. To split a column into multiple columns, simply click anywhere within that column and then go to the Paragraph section of the Home tab and click on the arrow next to the Add or Remove Columns option. (This is the one in the center of the bottom row of that section that shows two sets of lines side by side with a dropdown arrow on the right-hand side.)

You can choose between One Column, Two Columns, Three Columns, or More Columns.

To split a list of values into two columns, select Two Columns. To change a list that is in multiple columns back to a single column, choose One Column.

When you click on More Columns you can specify not only the number of columns, but the spacing between them.

The way multiple columns work is that PowerPoint will fill the first column completely before it moves on to putting text into the second column. This means you may have to use extra enters to get half of your list into the second column. Otherwise you may end up with a column with ten entries next to a column with two entries. Better to go to the seventh line in that list and enter until six of your entries are in the first column and six are in the second column.

(If that sounded confusing, just try it in PowerPoint and it'll make more sense.)

Change Spacing Between Lines of Text

If you want to change the amount of space that appears between lines of text, you can do so by going to the Paragraph section of the Home tab and clicking on the arrow next to the Line Spacing option. This is the one with up and down arrows on the left-hand side of a group of lines that is located in the center of the top row.

Click on the arrow to see the available options, but be careful because it applies that space to any lines you have, even ones you might want to keep together.

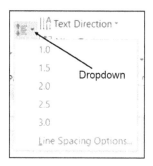

Your other, and perhaps better, option is to right-click and choose Paragraph from the dropdown menu. This will bring up the Paragraph dialogue box. In the Spacing section you can specify the size of the space before and after each paragraph. This can be a way of putting space between bullet points or paragraphs while keeping the lines within a bullet point or paragraph close together.

Bullets and Numbering

By default, most of the templates include bullets within the main body of each presentation slide. If you want to change the type of bullet, turn off bullets for a specific line, add a bullet to a specific line, or change the bullets to numbers, then you can do so with the Bullets and Numbering options in the top left corner of the Paragraph section of the Home tab.

To change the type of bullet, click on the row you want to change or highlight all of your rows if there's more than one, and then go to the Bullets option (the one with dots next to lines in the top left corner of the Paragraph section of the Home tab) and click on the dropdown arrow.

You'll see a box around the type of bullet that's currently being used. Click on None if you don't want a bulleted list. Or click on one of the other options if you want to change the type of bullet. You can hold your cursor over each option to see what it will look like before you make your selection.

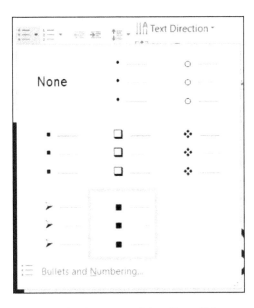

Clicking on Bullets and Numbering at the bottom of that list will let you specify the size of the bullet relative to the text as well as the color of the bullet. (But remember that the more you customize things, the more work you have to do throughout your presentation to keep everything uniform.)

If you want a numbered or lettered list instead (e.g., 1, 2, 3 or A, B, C) then click on the Numbering dropdown. There you can see a list of available numbered list options to choose from.

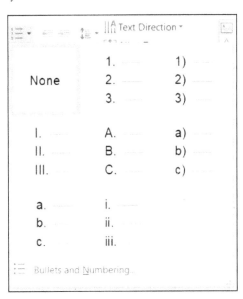

If you need to start at a number other than 1 or a letter other than A, click on Bullets and Numbering at the bottom of the list and then choose your starting point using the Start At box in the bottom right. For lettered lists (A, B, C) you enter a position number and it will change the letter. So a 1 equals A, a 2 equals B, etc. As with the bulleted list, you can also change the relative size of the number or letter compared to the list and change the color of the letter or number.

Another option for changing bullets or numbering is to right-click and go to either Bullets or Numbering in the dropdown menu.

Format Painter

If you ever find yourself in a situation where the formatting on one section of your presentation or your slide doesn't match another and you just want to take the formatting from one of the two and transfer it to the other, then the Format Painter is the easiest way to do so. It's located in the Clipboard section of the Home tab and looks like a little hand broom to me. (Given the name it's obviously a paintbrush.)

To use it, first highlight the text that's formatted the way you want. Next, click on the Format Painter. Then highlight the text that you want to be formatted that way. The formatting should transfer over, including font, font size, font color, line spacing, and type of bulleting/numbering.

Do not click anywhere else in between those steps and do not try to use the arrows to move between sections of text. Highlight, click, highlight. (Otherwise you might carry the formatting to the wrong text.)

This tool can be a lifesaver if someone has done weird things in a presentation you're trying to fix.

If the result isn't what you wanted or expected, then use Ctrl + Z to undo it and try again. Sometimes with paragraphs of text it can matter whether you selected the initial paragraph from the beginning or from the end. So if the formatting didn't transfer the way you thought it should, try selecting from the bottom of the paragraph up instead.

If you have more than one place you want to transfer formatting to, you can double-click on the Format Painter tool and then click on all of the text you want to change. It will stay selected until you click on it once more or hit Esc.

Other

As with formatting text you'll notice that there were a couple paragraph formatting options I didn't cover here. (SmartArt and Text Direction). If you do find yourself wanting to use either option they're available in the Paragraph section of the Home tab, but they shouldn't be needed for a basic presentation.

ADDING A TABLE TO A
PRESENTATION SLIDE

Now that we've covered how to add text to your presentation and then format it, let's discuss how to add a table of data or a picture to your presentation.

If you look at a blank content slide that hasn't had any text added to it yet, you'll see in the center of the text box for most of these slides that there's a series of images. This is from a text box in a Two Content slide:

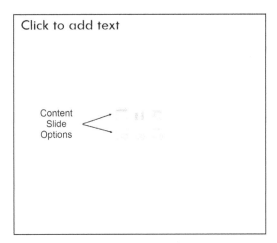

These are options you have other than just typing text into that box. Your options are Insert Table, Insert Chart, Insert a SmartArt Graphic, Pictures, Online Pictures, and Insert Video.

Once you choose one of these options you can't then type in that area. It's one or the other. (Although you could add a text box to the slide and put in text that way if you wanted. That's intermediate-level so we're not going to cover it here but the option can be found on the Insert tab in the Text section.)

We're not going to cover all of the non-text options in this guide, just adding a table and inserting a picture.

Let's start with the table option.

Insert Your Table

The first option in that set of images is to Insert Table.

Click on it and you'll see the Insert Table dialogue box. It lets you specify the number of columns and rows you want in your inserted table.

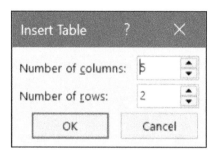

After you've chosen how many columns and rows you want, PowerPoint will insert a blank table with that number of columns and rows into that text box in your presentation. The first row will be formatted as a header row (so in a different color).

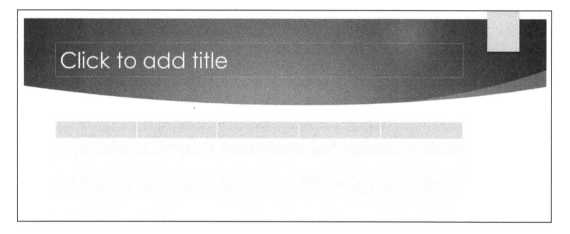

You can then click into any cell in that table to add your information. The colors used to create the table will match the theme you're using.

(If you look at each theme you'll see a set of colored squares at the bottom of the image for that theme. Those are the colors that are used for text, bullets, tables, and SmartArt for that theme. You can change that if you want under the Design tab under Table Tools, but the purpose of a theme is to use a coherent color scheme that all works together.)

Adding Text or Numbers to Your Table

To add text or numbers to your table, just go to the cell in the table where you want to add your text and start typing. If you enter text that is wider than the width of the column, it will automatically go to the next line and the row height will change to make sure all of the text is visible.

If you have the information in an existing table in Word or Excel, you can copy the information from that table into PowerPoint by highlighting the cells in Word or Excel, using copy (Ctrl + C), and then clicking into the first cell in the PowerPoint table where you want to place that information and using paste (Ctrl + V).

(This is sometimes the easier option when you have a lot of number formatting to do.)

Aligning Text Within Cells

If after you've entered text into your table you want to change the alignment of the text so that it's centered or left-aligned, etc. you can do this by highlighting the cells you want to change, going to the Layout tab under Table Tools, and going to the Alignment section. The top row where you see the three options with lines is where you can choose to left-align, center, or right-align text. The second row where you see the three boxes with lines in them is where you can choose to place text at the top, center, or bottom of each cell.

Adding Additional Rows or Columns

If you add a table and then want additional rows added to the table, simply use the tab key from the last cell in the last row of the table and PowerPoint will add a new line.

You can also highlight a row, go to the Layout tab under Table Tools, and choose Insert Above or Insert Below from the Rows & Columns section to add a row.

To add a column, highlight an existing column, go to the Layout tab under Table Tools, and choose Insert Left or Insert Right from the Rows & Columns section.

You can also highlight a row or column and right-click to bring up the mini formatting bar which has an Insert option with a dropdown arrow for inserting rows and columns.

Deleting a Row or Column

To delete a row or column from a table that you've decided you don't want, you can highlight the row or column, right-click and choose Cut or use the Delete option on the mini formatting bar.

Or you can click into a cell in that row or column, go to the Layout section of Table Tools, and under the Rows & Columns section click on the dropdown arrow under Delete. From there you can choose Delete Columns, Delete Rows, or Delete Table.

Deleting the Table

To delete the entire table, right-click and use the Delete option in the mini formatting bar to choose Delete Table. Or right-click on the table and choose Select Table from the dropdown and then use the Delete or Backspace key.

Or hold your mouse over the edge of the table until it looks like a four-sided arrow. Click on the table to select it and then use the Delete key or the Backspace key to delete it.

Moving the Table

Click on the table to select it or right-click and choose Select Table. Hold your mouse over the edge of the table until it looks like a four-sided arrow and then left-click and drag the table to where you want it.

Changing Column Width

To change the width of a column, click on a cell in the column and go to the Layout section of Table Tools and change the value in the Cell Size section for the Width.

You can also hold your mouse over the right-hand side of the column in the table itself until the cursor looks like two parallel lines with arrows pointing off to the sides and then left-click and drag to your desired width or double-left click to get the column to automatically resize to the width of the text that's currently in that column.

When you change the column width under Table Tools it will change just that column's width, so will also change the size of the table. Same with double-clicking to change the column width. If you use the click and drag option, both that column and the one next to it will have their column width changed but the overall size of the table will stay the same. That also means you can only click and drag so far because you'll be limited by the width of the two columns.

Changing Row Height

To change the height of a row, click on a cell in the row and go to the Layout section of Table Tools and change the value in the Cell Size section for the Height.

You can also hold your mouse over the bottom edge of the row in the table itself until the cursor looks like two parallel lines with arrows pointing up and down and then left-click and drag to your desired height. You will be limited in how skinny you can make a row based upon the font size for the text in the table.

With both methods, just that row's height will change so the table height will change as well.

Resizing the Table

To change the dimensions of an entire table, you can click on the table and then left-click and drag from any of the white squares around the edge of the table. Be sure that you have a white double-sided arrow when you do so or you may just ended up moving the table around. Clicking on one of the white boxes in the corner will allow you to resize the table proportionately as long as you click and drag at an angle.

You can also click on the table and go to the Layout tab under Table Tools and change the dimensions for the table listed under the Table Size section. If you want to resize the table and have the relative height and width of the table stay the same, click the Lock Aspect Ratio box first. When you do that PowerPoint will adjust both measurements at once to keep the ratio of height to width for the table constant.

Splitting Cells in a Table

You can take one or more cells in a table and split them into multiple cells. To do this, highlight the cell or cells you want to split, go to the Layout tab under Table Tools, and click on Split Cells in the Merge section. This will bring up the Split Cells dialogue box which lets you specify how many columns and rows you want each cell split into. This applies to each cell you selected. So if you select four cells and tell it to split them into two columns and one row, each of those four cells will be split into two columns and one row, so you'll have eight cells where there were four before.

You can also bring up the Split Cells dialogue box by highlighting the cells you want to split, right-clicking, and choosing Split Cells from the dropdown menu.

Merging Cells in a Table

You can also merge cells in a table. In this case, highlight the cells that you want to merge into one cell, go to the Layout tab under Table Tools, go to the Merge section, and choose Merge Cells.

You could also select the cells you want to merge, right-click, and choose Merge Cells from the dropdown menu.

ADDING A PICTURE TO A
PRESENTATION SLIDE

The option directly below Insert Table is Pictures. Click on it and you'll see the Insert Picture dialogue box. By default it will open in your Pictures folder on your computer, but you can navigate from there to any location on your computer where the picture you want is stored. If you click on the All Pictures dropdown option next to the File Name box you can see the picture file types that PowerPoint will accept. (Which looks to be pretty much any type you can image.)

Navigate to where the picture you want is saved, click on the picture, and then choose Insert.

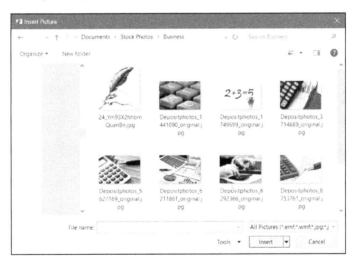

(There is an option there to link instead of insert your photo, but I'd advise against it because it's far too easy to break a link like that. Better to just put the image into your presentation.)

The image will insert into your slide at a size that fits within the text box where you chose to insert it. If the image is smaller than the active area it will insert at its current size, but if it's larger than the active area it will be scaled down and possibly cropped to fit.

(This is for when you use the Pictures icon to insert an image into a text box. You can also go to the Insert tab and choose Pictures from the Images section there to insert a picture on a blank slide.

In that case the image you insert will be centered in the presentation slide and may fit the entire slide if it's large enough.)

Moving a Picture

Once your image has been inserted into your slide, you can click on the image and drag it to the location you want. Left-click anywhere on the image, hold down the left-click, and drag the image to its new location. (It will take the text box it was inserted into with it, but if you then delete the image, the text box will reappear in its original location.)

Resizing a Picture

You can also resize a picture after you insert it into your slide. If you have specific dimensions that you want to use, click on the image and go to the Format tab under Picture Tools. On the far right-hand side you'll see the Size section.

Change either the height or the width and the image will resize proportionately. (So PowerPoint will adjust the other measurement to keep the height to width ratio the same.)

You can also click onto the image and then left-click on any of the white boxes around the perimeter and drag until the image is the size you want. This will not resize the image proportionately, so you can easily end up with a distorted image if you do it this way. But if you click on a corner and drag at an angle that usually will work because you are resizing the image on both the horizontal and vertical dimensions at once. (If you don't like the result, remember, Ctrl + Z to undo.)

Rotating a Picture

If you want to rotate the picture that you inserted, click on the image and then click on the little white outline of an arrow circling to the right that's above the image.

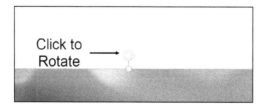

Click and hold this while you move your cursor in the direction you want to rotate the image and it will rotate along with your mouse.

Your other option is to click on the image and then go to the Format tab under Picture Tools and go to the Arrange section and choose Rotate. You can choose from the dropdown menu which lets you rotate 90 degrees right or left or flip the image vertically or horizontally. If you need more options than that, click on More Rotation Options to bring up the Format Picture task pane on the right-hand side of the screen. There you can set your rotation (the third option) to anything you want.

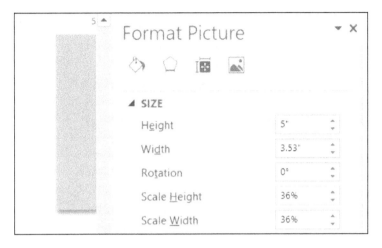

Cropping a Picture

Sometimes I'll drop a picture into a presentation and then realize that I didn't want the entire picture, I just wanted a section of it. (This is especially true when I take screenshots of Excel using Print Screen and then want to just keep a small section of that screenshot for my presentation.) In those cases, I need to crop the image to only show the portion I care about.

To crop an image, right-click on the image and choose Crop from the mini formatting bar. You should then see small black bars on each side of the image and at the corners. Left-click on those bars and drag until only the portion of the image that you want to keep is visible. Be sure when you click and drag that the cursor looks like a bar, because otherwise you might end up resizing the image instead. (If so, Ctrl + Z to undo and try again.)

When you move the boundaries of the image, you'll still see the full image but muted where it's no longer within your new boundaries.

You can click on the image and move it to make sure that the portion of the image you want to keep is within your new boundaries. (And if you insert an image that PowerPoint cropped and you want a different portion of that image to be visible, you can choose to "crop" the image and then click and drag until the portion of the image you wanted to be visible is, without actually changing the boundaries of the image.)

When you're satisfied that the cropped portion is what you want, hit Esc. You should now have just the cropped portion of the image.

Your other option for cropping is to go to the Format tab under Picture Tools and choose Crop from the Size section. The first option in the dropdown is a simple crop. You can also crop to a shape or crop to a specific aspect ratio.

Bring Forward/Send Backward

If you are ever in a situation where you have an image that overlaps a text box, you may need to use the bring forward or send backward options. These options determine which layer is visible when two layers overlap. If you have an image on top that you want in back, you send backward. If you have an image that's hidden that you need to move to the top you bring it forward.

Click on your image, go to the Format tab under Picture Tools, and go to the Arrange section. Choose either Bring Forward or Send Backward depending on what you need to do with the image. If there are multiple layers of images you can click on the arrow instead and choose to Bring to Front or Send to Back to make the image you've clicked the topmost layer or the backmost layer.

Alignment

Another option in the Arrange section of the Format tab is Align. There are a number of options available here. To align an image with respect to the presentation slide, click on the image and then click on the dropdown for Align.

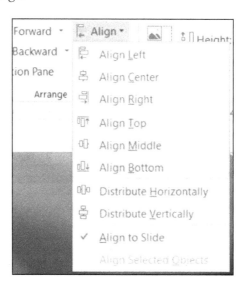

You can choose to align left (place the image along the left-hand side of the slide), align center (place the image in the center of the slide as judged from left to right), align right (place the image along the right-hand side of the slide), align top (place the image along the top edge of the slide), align middle (place the image in the center of the slide as judged from top to bottom), or align bottom (place the image along the bottom edge of the slide).

Distribute horizontally will center the image judged from left to right. Distribute vertically will center the image judged from top to bottom. Where this one matters is when you have multiple images selected at once. If you have multiple images selected at once then it will take those images and distribute them either across the width of the slide (horizontally) or from top to bottom (vertically) so that there is equal space between the images and the edges of the slide.

If you do have multiple images, you can select those images, and then under Align choose Align Selected Objects and instead of aligning the objects to the presentation slide it will align them to one another. So, for example, align right would move the left-hand object into alignment with the right-hand object.

Picture Styles

There is a Picture Styles section in the Format tab under Picture Tools. Click on your image to see what choices are available to you and then click on each style to see what it will look like in your slide. What these generally do is add borders or shading to your picture.

(I would recommend not using these unless you have a good reason to do so. I can't tell you how many times I've seen a presentation that had all sorts of added weirdness that distracted from what the presenter was trying to say. I'm a firm believer in keeping it simple.)

Adjusting a Picture

In the same way that I don't think you should use Picture Styles unless you need to, I'm going to advise against getting too fancy with adjusting a picture you import into your presentation, but I will point out the existence of the options for you. If you go to the Format tab under Picture Tools you'll see on the far left-hand side that there is a section called Adjust.

Click on the arrow under Corrections and you can see a series of options for sharpening or softening an image and for changing the brightness or contrast of the image. You can see what each option will look like as well.

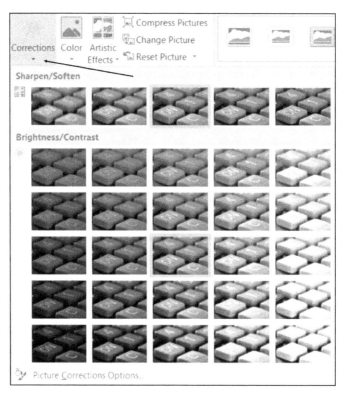

Click on the arrow under Color and you'll see that you can change the color saturation, color tone, or recolor your image.

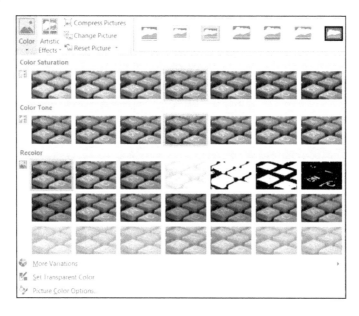

Click on the arrow under Artistic Effects and you'll see that you can apply a number of effects to your image.

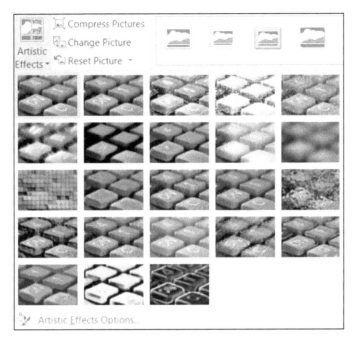

Once more, I wouldn't recommend doing this unless you have a good reason for doing so. Always ask yourself two questions before making a change like this. One, will it still look professional? (And professional means different things in different environments, so what's fine for an advertising agency will not be fine for an investment bank.) And, two, does what I just did make it easier for others to understand my presentation?

If it doesn't look professional, don't do it. And if it doesn't increase other people's ability to understand you, don't do it. The last thing you want is people more focused on what on earth that is than on what you're saying.

ANIMATIONS

If you have a presentation slide with multiple bullet points it's often very useful to have those bullet points appear one at a time. This way people listen to what you're saying instead of trying to read ahead on the slide and see what you're going to say.

The way you get one bullet point to appear on a slide at a time is by using the options under the Animations tab.

First, go to the slide where you want to add animation. Next, click on one of the lines of text and go to the Animations tab. From there click on one of the options in the Animation section.

I recommend using Appear. It simply shows the line without any fancy tricks which can be distracting.

If the slide you're dealing with is just a list of bullet points with no indents and no images, the lines in the slide should now be numbered starting at one and up to however many lines you have.

This is the order in which they're going to appear as you give your presentation. (Usually triggered by hitting Enter, using the down arrow on your keyboard, or left-clicking to advance through the slide as you present.)

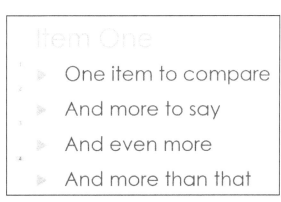

If you have indented lines of text you will probably need to fix their numbering. By default in my version of PowerPoint any indented lines share the numbering of their "parent" line. This is probably best understood visually. See below:

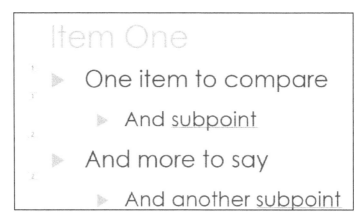

See how we have lines of text with indented lines below them? And how they are all numbered the same? So the first main line of text is 1 and so is its subpoint? And then the next is 2 and so is its subpoint?

That means the main line of text and the subpoint will appear in the presentation at the same time. But usually what I want is to make my main point and then make a subpoint.

To fix this, click into the slide, go to the Animations tab and click on the small arrow in the corner of the Animation section. This will bring up the Appear dialogue box.

Go to the Text Animation tab and change the Group Text option. Depending on how many levels of bullets you have on the slide you will probably need the "By 2nd Level Paragraphs" or the "By 3rd Level Paragraphs" option to get all lines of text to appear individually. Click on OK.

The slide should now show adjusted numbering based upon your choice.

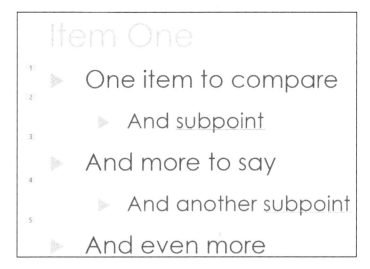

If you also have pictures in your slide, you need to be sure that the pictures are also going to appear or that it's okay that the picture appears first with no text. Also be careful to make sure that the picture appears in the order you want it.

If I have already numbered the lines of text in my slide and I click on a picture and then choose Appear from the Animation section of the Animations tab, it will be numbered last.

The easiest way to change the order in which your different elements appear on the slide is by going to the Animations tab and clicking on Animation Pane. This will bring up a pane on the right-hand side of the presentation slide that says Animation Pane.

It will show all of your elements and the order in which they appear. (You may have to click on the small double arrow under a numbered section to see all of your numbered options from your slide. In the image below I've already done that so clicking on it again would hide them.)

To change the order, click on one of the elements listed and then use the up and down arrows above the list of elements to move that element up or down.

You can also change the level at which your text is grouped in this pane by clicking on the arrow next to one of the text elements and then choosing Effect Options from the dropdown menu to bring up the Appear dialogue box. (Just remember that these choices are applied at the slide level, so any change you make in this manner will apply to all text elements on the slide.)

If you want to have some of your bullet points appear together but others appear separately, the best way I know to do this is to set up the slide as if everything will appear separately and then highlight the rows you want to appear together and click on your option in the Animation section of the Animations tab.

There are other things you can do with animation that we're not going to cover here, such as have each bullet point appear on its own on a timed schedule. But for this beginner guide I just wanted you to know how to structure your slides so that each point you want to make appears separately.

It's tempting to try to make a presentation more interesting with things like this, but if you can't engage your audience with what you're saying then fix what you're saying instead.

I would strongly urge you to keep to just using Appear as your animation option. You can have your bullet points fly in or even bounce in (please, no), but ask yourself if that's appropriate for your audience. If you're presenting to first graders, sure, have a bullet point bounce in. But a potential business client? Eh. Or a group of your professional peers? Uh-uh. Don't do it.

In a minute we'll talk about how to walk through your slides and see your animations in action, but first let's talk about a few general design principles I think are good to keep in mind.

BASIC DESIGN PRINCIPLES

I've touched on this a few times, but I think it's good to take a chapter and discuss some basic design principles to keep in mind as you're preparing your presentation. I'm going to assume here that you're actually intending to use your PowerPoint presentation as a presentation. Meaning, you're going to talk through it and not expect it to talk for you, and that the slides are going to be presented on a projector of some sort to a live audience.

(In other words, I'm not addressing the consulting model of using PowerPoint where you put together a weekly client presentation on a series of slides that you hand out to your client and pack full of information and then walk through even though the client could just read the darned things themselves without paying you thousands of dollars to be there while they do it.)

Font Size

Make sure that all of the text on your slide will be visible to anyone in the room. I'd try to have all of the text be 12 point or larger if you can manage it and with a strong preference for probably 16 point or above.

Font Type

As with all other design elements it can be tempting to use a fancy font. Resist the temptation. You want a basic, clear, easy-to-read font for your presentation elements. This means using something like Arial or Calibri or Times New Roman instead of something like Algerian or Comic Sans.

Summaries Instead of Explanations

The text on your slide should be there as a general outline of what you're going to say, not contain the full text of what you want to say. Think of each bullet point as a prompt that you can look at to trigger your recollection.

The reason you do it this way is because people will try to read whatever you put in front of them. So if you give them a slide full of text they will be busy reading that text rather than listening to what you have to say.

Also, if it's all on the slide, why listen to you at all?

So use the text on your slide as a high-level summary of your next point instead of as an explanation.

For example, I might have a slide titled "The Three Stages of Money Laundering" and then list on that slide three bullet points, "Placement", "Layering", and "Integration". As I show each bullet point I'll discuss what each of those stages is and how it works. If I feel a need to really go into detail then I'll have a separate slide for each one where I provide further information in small bite-sized chunks.

Contrast

You want your text to be visible. Which means you have to think about contrast. If you have a dark background, then use a light-colored text. For example, dark blue background, white text. If you have a light background, use a dark-colored text. For example, white background, black text.

And beware anything that could trip up someone with color-blindness. So no red on green or green on red and no blue on yellow or yellow on blue.

Also, and this may be more of a personal preference, but I try to use the slide templates that have white for the background behind the text portions of my slides. I'm fine with colorful borders and colorful header sections, but where the meat of the presentation is I prefer to have a white background often with black text. (That's the easiest combination to read.)

So I'll choose the Ion Boardroom theme before I'll choose the Ion theme, for example. That one's a perfect example.

Don't Get Cute

PowerPoint has a lot of bells and whistles. You can have lines of text that fly in and slide in and fade away. Or slides that flash in or appear through bars. And some of the templates it provides are downright garish.

Resist the urge to overdo it.

Ask yourself every time you're tempted to add some special effect if adding it will improve the effectiveness of your presentation. And ask yourself what your boss's boss's boss would think of your presentation. I've worked in banking and regulatory environments and I will tell you there is little appreciation in those environments for overly-bright colors and flashy special effects. (Whereas some tech company environment where the CEO wears jeans and t-shirts to work may be all for that kind of thing. Know your audience.)

I do think that using the animation option to have one bullet point appear at a time is a good idea. But you can do that with the Appear option. You don't need Fade, Fly In, Float In, Split, Wipe, etc.

And, yes, it can sometimes feel boring to use the same animation for a hundred slides in a row. But remember the point of your presentation is to convey information to your audience. Anything that doesn't help you do that should go.

ADDING NOTES TO A SLIDE

Now that we've walked through the basics of creating your presentation, let's cover a few other things you might want to do, starting with adding notes to your slides. You can print a notes version of the slides that lets you see each slide as well as your notes. This is a great approach when you have something very specific you want to say but that you don't want to put in the text of the slide.

So how do you add them?

In my version of PowerPoint the Notes portion of the presentation is not visible by default. But at the bottom of the slide I'm viewing there is the word Notes along the bottom border. If I click on this it reduces the size of the main slide and shows me a gray box that says "Click to add notes." If I click into that space and start typing those notes will go on the notes section for that slide.

The other option is to go to the Show section of the View tab and click on Notes. This will also reduce the size of the presentation slide and show the "Click to add notes" section.

Once the Notes section is visible you can click on the same option again to hide it.

OTHER TIPS AND TRICKS

Now that you understand the basics of putting together a PowerPoint presentation, let's discuss a few things you can do in PowerPoint that weren't covered elsewhere but that I think are worth knowing about as a beginning user.

Spellcheck

It's always a good idea to run spellcheck on anything you create for an audience. To check the spelling in your document, go to the Proofing section of the Review tab and click on Spelling. (It's on the far left-hand side.)

PowerPoint will then walk through your entire document flagging spelling errors and repeated words. For each one it will show you its suggested changes on the right-hand side of the screen and will highlight in the presentation slides the word that was flagged as having an error.

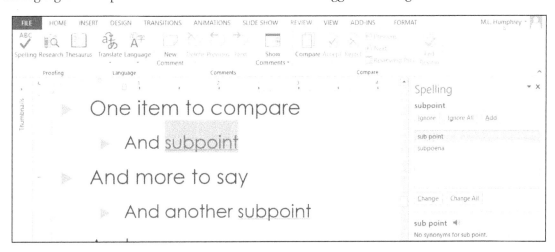

If you don't want to make the suggested change, click on Ignore. If PowerPoint has flagged a word, such as an unusual name, that is used multiple times throughout the document and you want it to ignore all uses of that word, you can choose Ignore All. (You can also choose Add to place it into your dictionary, but be careful with that because it will be added for all documents and that may not be what you want.)

For spelling errors PowerPoint will suggest possible words that you meant. Click on the word in the list that is the correct spelling and choose Change. If you're really bold you could do Change All and all misspellings of that word will be changed throughout the document, just be sure that's what you want.

Find

If you need to find a specific reference in your slides you can use Find to do so. The Find option can be found in the Editing section of the Home tab (on the far right-hand side). Click on Find and the Find dialogue box will appear.

You can also open the Find dialogue box by using Ctrl + F.

Type the word you want into the white text box and then click on Find Next. PowerPoint will walk you through the entire document moving to the next instance of that word each time you click on Find Next.

By clicking the boxes under the search term box, you can choose to just search for whole words only or to just search for words with the same capitalization (match case). This is useful with Find, but essential with Replace.

Replace Text

If you need to replace text within your slides you can use Replace. This essentially pairs the Find option with an option that takes the word you were searching for and replaces it with another. You can either launch the Replace dialogue box by using Ctrl + H or by going to the Editing section of the Home tab and clicking on Replace.

When you do this you'll see the Replace dialogue box. It has a text box for the text you want to find and a text box for what you want to replace that text with.

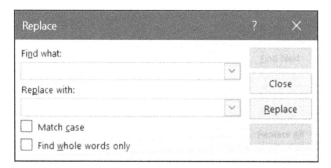

Once you've completed both boxes, click on Replace All to replace all instances of that word in your document. (Replace, when available, will replace only the next usage of the word.) If you don't complete the "replace with" box then you'll be deleting the text you chose to find.

With this one I strongly urge you to use match case and find whole words only. For example, let's say you wanted to replace the name Dan with Bob. Maybe Dan got fired and Bob took his place. (Bear with me, this is just to illustrate a point.) If you don't match case, then PowerPoint will replace every usage of dan with bob. That's probably not going to be a big issue, but if you don't look for whole words only then PowerPoint will take every dan in every word in your presentation and replace it with bob. So, for example, "danger" would become "bobger".

Replacing text is easy to do and easy to mess up. Be very, very careful if you choose to use it.

Replace Font

PowerPoint has a replace function that is unique to it and also incredibly useful. If you go to the Editing section of the Home tab and click on the dropdown arrow next to Replace you'll see that there is an option there to Replace Fonts.

Click on that option to bring up the Replace Font dialogue box.

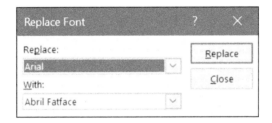

It will show you two dropdown menus.

The first menu is where you select the font that is in your presentation that you want to replace. It should only show the fonts used in your presentation. (Although it also kept showing me Arial whether it was used in the template or not and even after I'd replaced it with another font using the Replace font option.)

The second menu is where you choose the font you want to replace that font with. Once you do this and click on Replace, every usage of the first font will be replaced with the second font. This can come in very handy if you have a corporate requirement to use a specific font that wasn't followed when the presentation was created.

Just be sure to then look back through your presentation and make sure everything looks "right", because different fonts will take up different amounts of space on the page and it's possible that changing over the font could impact the appearance of your slides.

Presentation Size

PowerPoint gives you the choice between two presentation sizes. The standard size is 4:3 and the widescreen size is 16:9. You can also choose a custom slide size.

All of these choices are available in the Customize section of the Design tab on the far right side where it says Slide Size. Click on the dropdown arrow to make your choice.

(If you click on the Custom Slide Size option you can even make a presentation that is in portrait orientation, so like a normal printed report, rather than in landscape orientation. Although, if you're going to do this do it before you start putting together your slides or you'll have a complete mess to fix up. This would not be a good choice for a presentation that's going to be projected on a screen, but could be an interesting idea for a printed presentation.)

PRESENTING YOUR SLIDES

When it comes time to do your presentation, chances are someone will hook up a laptop with your presentation on it to a projector. By default that will show your computer screen. But you don't want someone to see what you've been seeing this whole time as you built your presentation. You just want them to see the slides and nothing else.

So when it comes time to present you need to go into presentation mode in PowerPoint.

To do this, go to the Slide Show tab.

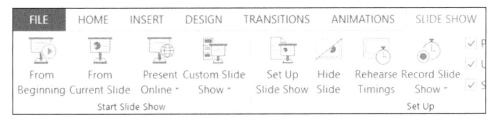

On the left-hand side you have the Start Slide Show section. If you click on From Beginning, this will start a presentation at the first slide in your PowerPoint presentation. If you click on From Current Slide it will start the presentation at the slide that's currently visible.

F5 will also start your presentation from the beginning. And Shift + F5 will start your presentation from your current slide.

Either choice will launch the slides you've created as a full-screen presentation.

The PowerPoint screen you've been working in will still be there and open behind the scenes. You can reach it using Alt + Tab to move through your active windows or you can use Esc to close the presentation version.

To navigate forward through the slides in your presentation, use the down arrow on the keyboard, Enter, or left-click. If you've added animations to your presentation then you'll move forward one animated section at a time. If not you'll move forward one slide at a time.

To move backward, use the up arrow on the keyboard. You can also right-click and choose Previous from the dropdown menu.

Before you enter presentation mode, I'd recommend having any additional windows you're going to want open already so you can easily access them using Alt + Tab.

And it's always a good idea to run through your presentation slides before you present to anyone so you can check and make sure that all the animations, etc. are working. You can do this on your computer screen easily enough by using F5 or the option to view the slideshow from the beginning.

Also—and I hesitate to mention this just because of the potential for things to go wrong and you to not be able to fix them in front of a crowd—there is an option to view your slides in Presenter View. What this is supposed to do is show on your computer screen the slide the audience can currently see as well as your slide notes and the next slide.

But there's a potential to accidentally display that information up on the screen for the audience instead. If that happens, at the top of the screen there is an option at the top of the presenter screen to choose Display Settings and then Swap Presenter View and Slide Show.

If you want to try using Presenter View, right-click on your slide when in presentation mode and choose Show Presenter View from the dropdown menu.

To close a presentation, hit Esc. Or right-click and choose End Show from the dropdown menu.

PRINTING YOUR PRESENTATION

To print your presentation, handouts, or slides with notes, you can type Ctrl + P or go to the File tab and then choose Print on the left-hand side. Both choices will bring you to the same location.

You have a number of print options on the left-hand side and then a preview of what the page will look like when you print it on the right-hand side.

The default is to print all of your slides and in full-page format and that's what your preview will show. But let's walk through everything you can see on this page and your other possible print options.

Print

Right at the top of the page under the Print header is the printer icon. It shows a printer and says Print under it. This is what you click when you're ready to print your document.

Copies

Next to that is where you specify the number of copies to print. By default the number to print is 1, but you can use the arrows on the right-hand side of the text box to increase that number. (Or decrease it if you've already increased it.) You can also just click into the white text box and type the number of copies you need.

Printer

Below those two options is the Printer section. This is where you specify the printer to use. It should be your default printer, but in some corporate environments you'll want to change your printer choice if, for example, you need the color printer.

To do this, click on the arrow on the right-hand side. This will bring up a dropdown menu with all of your printers listed. Click on the one you want. If the one you want isn't listed then use Add Printer to add it.

Printer Properties

If you want to print on both sides of the page you'll need to specify this using Printer Properties which is the blue text visible under the name of the printer. Clicking on that text will bring up a Document Properties dialogue box.

Click on the Layout tab and choose from the dropdown under Print on Both Sides to choose whether to print on both sides of the page and how. If the paper orientation is Portrait, choose Flip on Long Edge. If the paper orientation is Landscape, choose Flip on Short Edge.

You don't need to change the other properties here because they're available on the main screen.

Print All Slides/Print Selection/Print Current Slide/Custom Range

Your next option is what to print. By default, you'll print all the slides in the presentation.

If you were clicked onto a specific slide in the presentation and want to just print it then you can choose Print Current Slide. (When you choose this the print preview should change to show just that one slide.)

If you had selected more than one slide in the presentation and then chose to print, you can choose Print Selection to print those slides.

Your other option is print a custom range. The easiest way to use this one is to type the slide numbers you want into the Slides text box directly below the dropdown. This will automatically change the dropdown selection to Custom Range. Your preview will also change to just show the slides you've listed.

You can list numbers either individually or as ranges. If you list a range you use a dash between the first and last number. So 1-10 would print slides 1 through 10. You can also use commas to separate numbers or ranges. So 1, 2, 5-12 would print slides 1, 2 and 5 through 12.

Full Page Slides/Notes Pages/Outline/Handouts

The next choice is what you want to print.

In the top section you can choose to print full page slides, notes pages, or an outline.

Full page slides will put one slide on each page you print and nothing else.

Notes pages will put one slide per page on the top half of the page and your notes on the bottom half of the page. Each page will be in portrait orientation. (Short edge on the top.)

Outline will take all of the text from your slides and list it out in the same way it's listed on the slides. So if there are bullet points, the outline will have them, too. If there aren't, it won't. Each printed page will contain multiple slides' worth of information. No images are included.

If you want to provide handout slides, you have a number of options to choose from. The one slide option will center each presentation slide in the middle of a page in portrait orientation. (Not recommended.) The two slide option will put two slides on each page in portrait orientation. (This is a good choice for handouts because it's still visible but doesn't waste paper the way the one-slide option does.)

You can put as many as nine slides on the page, but before you do that think about how legible that will be for the end-user. If you have a lot of slides with images it might be fine, but if they have a lot of text on them or if people will need/want to take a lot of notes, no one is going to thank you for putting nine slides on a page.

The horizontal and vertical choices determine whether the slides are ordered across and then down (horizontal) or down and then across (vertical). I think, at least in the U.S., that most people would expect horizontal.

Collated/Uncollated

This only matters if you're printing more than one copy of the presentation. In that case, you need to decide if you want to print one full copy at a time x number of times (collated) or if you want to print x copies of page 1 and then x copies of page 2 and then x copies of page 3 and so on until you've printed all pages of your document (uncollated).

In general, I would recommend collated, which is also the default.

Portrait Orientation/Landscape Orientation

This determines whether what you've chosen to print prints with the long edge of the page at the top or the short end of the page at the top. In general, PowerPoint chooses this for you and does a good job of it. For example, outline should be portrait and full page slides should be landscape.

However, you might want to change this for the handout slides. For one slide, four slide, and nine slide printing, I think landscape is a better choice than portrait. You can judge for yourself by looking at the preview and seeing how large the slides are and how much white space is taken up with each orientation.

Color/Grayscale/Pure Black and White

This option lets you choose whether to print your slides in color or not. The choice you make will probably depend on your available print resources. When you change the option you'll see in the print preview what each one looks like. The grayscale and pure black and white options seem to strip colored backgrounds out of the presentation. The pure black and white one strips color out of the header sections as well.

Edit Header & Footer

At the very bottom of the list you can click on the text Edit Header & Footer to bring up the Header and Footer dialogue box where you can choose to add the date and time, slide number, or a customized footer display to your printed document

Only the Notes and Handouts slides can have a header on them and that's specified on a separate tab.

Once you choose to apply your choices, you can see how it will look in the print preview.

WHERE TO LOOK
FOR OTHER ANSWERS

My goal in this guide was to give you a solid understanding of how PowerPoint works and the tools to create a basic presentation. But there are a number of topics I didn't cover in this guide, such as how to change a presentation slide background color, creating a custom design template, adding timing to your presentation slides, or adding objects or text boxes to a slide.

At some point you'll probably want to learn about one of these things.

So how do you do it? Where do you get these answers?

First, in PowerPoint itself you have a few options. You can hold your cursor over the choices in any of the tabs and you'll usually see a brief explanation of what that choice can do. For example, here is the New Slide option in the Home tab:

You can see that it says this option will let you "add a slide to your presentation." If that brief description isn't enough, a lot of the options have a Tell Me More option below that. Click on that text and the built-in Help function in PowerPoint will open giving a more detailed description of what you can do.

Another option is to go directly to the built-in Help function. You do this by clicking on the question mark in the top right corner of the screen or pressing F1. This will launch PowerPoint Help. From there you can either navigate to what you want or type in a search phrase in the search box.

I often find myself needing more information than this so turn to the internet. If I need to know the mechanics of how something works, the Microsoft website is the best option. For example, if I wanted to understand more about the colors used in each theme in PowerPoint I might search for "colors powerpoint theme microsoft 2013".

It's key that you add the powerpoint, microsoft, and your version year in your search.

When I get my search results, I then look for a search result that goes to support.office.com. There will usually be one in the top three or four search results.

If that doesn't work or I need to know something that isn't about how things work but can I do something, (and this is more true probably in Excel than in PowerPoint), then I will do an internet search to find a blog or user forum where someone else had the same question. Often there are good tutorials out there that you can read or watch to find your answer.

And, of course, you can also just reach out to me at mlhumphreywriter@gmail.com.

I don't check that email daily but I do check it regularly and I'm happy to track down an answer for you or point you in the right direction.

CONCLUSION

So there you have it. We've covered the basics of PowerPoint and at this point in time you should be able to create your own nicely polished basic presentation.

PowerPoint is great for presentations. And it's a valuable skill to have. I've used PowerPoint both in my corporate career as well as my writing career. If you're going to stand in front of a room of fifty (or five hundred) people it's nice to have a presentation up on a screen to help you stay focused on what you meant to say. (And it keeps you from staring down at a podium the whole time while you read your notes.)

It also gives your audience something to look at other than you.

Having said that, you'll have seen in this guide that I have some definite opinions about how PowerPoint presentations can be misused and abused. It can be fun to put a ton of crazy colors and shapes into your presentation and have things bouncing in and zooming out and flashing around, but resist that temptation.

Remember that PowerPoint is a tool, and that its purpose is to help you convey information to your audience. Anything you do in your presentation that takes away from your ability to convey information is a bad thing.

So exercise restraint. (Unless you're in a setting where a lack of restraint will help you, like a presentation to three hundred first graders…In that case, go wild.)

Anyway. Good luck with it. And reach out if you get stuck. I'm happy to help.

ABOUT THE AUTHOR

M.L. Humphrey is a former stockbroker with a degree in Economics from Stanford and an MBA from Wharton who has spent close to twenty years as a regulator and consultant in the financial services industry.

You can reach M.L. at mlhumphreywriter@gmail.com or at mlhumphrey.com.